Praise for Blueberry Delights Cookbook

A Collection of Blueberry Recipes
Cookbook Delights Series-Book 2

…"As we begin to understand more about the powerful antioxidants and vitamins found in blueberries, it's no wonder that this book is a natural selection.

Blueberry Delights Cookbook is a well-organized collection of recipes—versatile and traditional, as well as some fresh favorites. It's a great source to draw from when you're trying to eat healthier without sacrificing flavor. I'm partial to the *Cornbread Sticks with Blueberries, Blueberry Salsa,* and *Salmon with Blueberry Horseradish Sauce.*

Just talking about it makes me salivate!"…

Kimberly Carter
Publicist

…"Since 2005, blueberries have been named among the super fruits, having nutrient richness, antioxidant strength, and outstanding health benefits. It is no wonder that Whispering Pine Press International has added *Blueberry Delights* to the abundant and ever-growing *Cookbook Delights Series.* Over 240 fanciful and delicious recipes, phenomenal tidbits and informational pages, impressive and imaginative poetry promise to inspire and please the poet and the cook in you."…

Mary Scripture
Graphic Designer

Praise for Blueberry Delights Cookbook

A Collection of Blueberry Recipes
Cookbook Delights Series-Book 2

…"**Blueberry Delights Cookbook** is one book that makes my mouth water. Out of all the berries, blueberries are my favorite. With over 240 recipes, I'm sure to find plenty to tickle my taste buds.

Blueberry Delights complements the recipes with poetry and other useful information.

If you haven't yet purchased a book in this series, make *Blueberry Delights* the first. If you have already started this collection, you won't want to miss out on this delightful addition."…

Ed Archambeault
Spokane, WA

…"**Blueberry Delights** is a great cookbook because it not only includes over 240 recipes, but it also contains information and facts on nutrition, health, and cultivation to support the recipes. Reading the 'Did You Know' facts is fascinating, and the poetry by the author is an added extra feature that you won't find included in other cookbooks. **Blueberry Delights** is definitely a great value because it is packed with rich information. It makes an interesting book to read as well as a resourceful cookbook with delicious-tasting recipes arranged for easy use. I highly recommend this book to give as a gift."…

Dr. James G. Hood
Editor

Praise for Blueberry Delights Cookbook

A Collection of Blueberry Recipes
Cookbook Delights Series-Book 2

…"As with all of Hood's cookbooks, it is the extras that make **Blueberry Delights** truly stand out. At the beginning of the book, not only will you find a selection of Hood's themed poetry, but information about identifying different types of blueberry, which will be invaluable for those who like to go berry-picking; tips about growing and cultivating blueberries in your garden; and a fascinating introduction to the berry's history and folklore. Also present are the helpful metric conversion chart and glossary that will provide excellent assistance for less experienced cooks.

My family tried out the 'Blueberry Chicken Salsa Torte,' 'Multigrain Blueberry Pilaf,' and 'Oatmeal Blueberry Cookies.' Both the torte and the pilaf were longer, more involved recipes than we usually make on a weekday, but both were well worth the extra effort. The torte was simply amazing, the blueberry salsa a bright, flavorful twist that added the perfect touch. The torte recipe is very versatile and will easily accommodate delicious additions like roasted red peppers and pico de gallo for those who want to add their own flair. Although listed in the Appetizer section, it would also make a fun lunch item."…

Kim Saunders

Blueberry Delights Cookbook

A Collection of Blueberry Recipes

Cookbook Delights Series-Book 2

Karen Jean Matsko Hood

Current and Future Cookbooks
By Karen Jean Matsko Hood

DELIGHTS SERIES

Almond Delights
Anchovy Delights
Apple Delights
Apricot Delights
Artichoke Delights
Asparagus Delights
Avocado Delights
Banana Delights
Barley Delights
Basil Delights
Bean Delights
Beef Delights
Beer Delights
Beet Delights
Blackberry Delights
Blueberry Delights
Bok Choy Delights
Boysenberry Delights
Brazil Nut Delights
Broccoli Delights
Brussels Sprouts Delights
Buffalo Berry Delights
Butter Delights
Buttermilk Delights
Cabbage Delights
Calamari Delights
Cantaloupe Delights
Caper Delights
Cardamom Delights
Carrot Delights
Cashew Delights
Cauliflower Delights
Celery Delights
Cheese Delights
Cherry Delights
Chestnut Delights
Chicken Delights
Chili Pepper Delights
Chive Delights
Chocolate Delights

Chokecherry Delights
Cilantro Delights
Cinnamon Delights
Clam Delights
Clementine Delights
Coconut Delights
Coffee Delights
Conch Delights
Corn Delights
Cottage Cheese Delights
Crab Delights
Cranberry Delights
Cucumber Delights
Cumin Delights
Curry Delights
Date Delights
Edamame Delights
Egg Delights
Eggplant Delights
Elderberry Delights
Endive Delights
Fennel Delights
Fig Delights
Filbert (Hazelnut) Delights
Fish Delights
Garlic Delights
Ginger Delights
Ginseng Delights
Goji Berry Delights
Grape Delights
Grapefruit Delights
Grapple Delights
Guava Delights
Ham Delights
Hamburger Delights
Herb Delights
Herbal Tea Delights
Honey Delights
Honeyberry Delights
Honeydew Delights
Horseradish Delights

Huckleberry Delights
Jalapeño Delights
Jerusalem Artichoke Delights
Jicama Delights
Kale Delights
Kiwi Delights
Kohlrabi Delights
Lavender Delights
Leek Delights
Lemon Delights
Lentil Delights
Lettuce Delights
Lime Delights
Lingonberry Delights
Lobster Delights
Loganberry Delights
Macadamia Nut Delights
Mango Delights
Marionberry Delights
Milk Delights
Mint Delights
Miso Delights
Mushroom Delights
Mussel Delights
Nectarine Delights
Oatmeal Delights
Olive Delights
Onion Delights
Orange Delights
Oregon Berry Delights
Oyster Delights
Papaya Delights
Parsley Delights
Parsnip Delights
Pea Delights
Peach Delights
Peanut Delights
Pear Delights
Pecan Delights
Pepper Delights
Persimmon Delights
Pine Nut Delights
Pineapple Delights
Pistachio Delights

Plum Delights
Pomegranate Delights
Pomelo Delights
Popcorn Delights
Poppy Seed Delights
Pork Delights
Potato Delights
Prickly Pear Cactus Delights
Prune Delights
Pumpkin Delights
Quince Delights
Quinoa Delights
Radish Delights
Raisin Delights
Raspberry Delights
Rhubarb Delights
Rice Delights
Rose Delights
Rosemary Delights
Rutabaga Delights
Salmon Delights
Salmonberry Delights
Salsify Delights
Savory Delights
Scallop Delights
Seaweed Delights
Serviceberry Delights
Sesame Delights
Shallot Delights
Shrimp Delights
Soybean Delights
Spinach Delights
Squash Delights
Star Fruit Delights
Strawberry Delights
Sunflower Seed Delights
Sweet Potato Delights
Swiss Chard Delights
Tangerine Delights
Tapioca Delights
Tayberry Delights
Tea Delights
Teaberry Delights
Thimbleberry Delights

Tofu Delights
Tomatillo Delights
Tomato Delights
Trout Delights
Truffle Delights
Tuna Delights
Turkey Delights
Turmeric Delights
Turnip Delights
Vanilla Delights
Walnut Delights
Wasabi Delights
Watermelon Delights
Wheat Delights
Wild Rice Delights
Yam Delights
Yogurt Delights
Zucchini Delights

CITY DELIGHTS
Chicago Delights
Coeur d'Alene Delights
Great Falls Delights
Honolulu Delights
Minneapolis Delights
Phoenix Delights
Portland Delights
Sandpoint Delights
Scottsdale Delights
Seattle Delights
Spokane Delights
St. Cloud Delights

FOSTER CARE
Foster Children Cookbook
  and Activity Book
Foster Children's Favorite Recipes
Holiday Cookbook for
  Foster Families

GENERAL THEME
  DELIGHTS
Appetizer Delights
Baby Food Delights

Barbeque Delights
Beer-Making Delights
Beverage Delights
Biscotti Delights
Bisque Delights
Blender Delights
Bread Delights
Bread Maker Delights
Breakfast Delights
Brunch Delights
Cake Delights
Campfire Food Delights
Candy Delights
Canned Food Delights
Cast Iron Delights
Cheesecake Delights
Chili Delights
Chowder Delights
Cocktail Delights
College Cooking Delights
Comfort Food Delights
Cookie Delights
Cooking for One Delights
Cooking for Two Delights
Cracker Delights
Crepe Delights
Crockpot Delights
Dairy Delights
Dehydrated Food Delights
Dessert Delights
Dinner Delights
Dutch Oven Delights
Foil Delights
Fondue Delights
Food Processor Delights
Fried Food Delights
Frozen Food Delights
Fruit Delights
Gelatin Delights
Grilled Delights
Hiking Food Delights
Ice Cream Delights
Juice Delights
Kid's Delights

Kosher Diet Delights
Liqueur-Making Delights
Liqueurs and Spirits Delights
Lunch Delights
Marinade Delights
Microwave Delights
Milk Shake and Malt Delights
Panini Delights
Pasta Delights
Pesto Delights
Phyllo Delights
Pickled Food Delights
Picnic Food Delights
Pizza Delights
Preserved Delights
Pudding and Custard Delights
Quiche Delights
Quick Mix Delights
Rainbow Delights
Salad Delights
Salsa Delights
Sandwich Delights
Sea Vegetable Delights
Seafood Delights
Smoothie Delights
Snack Delights
Soup Delights
Supper Delights
Tart Delights
Torte Delights
Tropical Delights
Vegan Delights
Vegetable Delights
Vegetarian Delights
Vinegar Delights
Wildflower Delights
Wine Delights
Winemaking Delights
Wok Delights

GIFTS-IN-A-JAR SERIES
Beverage Gifts-in-a-Jar
Christmas Gifts-in-a-Jar
Cookie Gifts-in-a-Jar

Gifts-in-a-Jar
Gifts-in-a-Jar Catholic
Gifts-in-a-Jar Christian
Holiday Gifts-in-a-Jar
Soup Gifts-in-a-Jar

HEALTH-RELATED DELIGHTS
Achalasia Diet Delights
Adrenal Health Diet Delights
Anti-Acid Reflux Diet Delights
Anti-Cancer Diet Delights
Anti-Inflammation Diet Delights
Anti-Stress Diet Delights
Arthritis Delights
Bone Health Diet Delights
Diabetic Diet Delights
Diet for Pink Delights
Fibromyalgia Diet Delights
Gluten-Free Diet Delights
Healthy Breath Diet Delights
Healthy Digestion Diet Delights
Healthy Heart Diet Delights
Healthy Skin Diet Delights
Healthy Teeth Diet Delights
High-Fiber Diet Delights
High-Iodine Diet Delights
High-Protein Diet Delights
Immune Health Diet Delights
Kidney Health Diet Delights
Lactose-Free Diet Delights
Liquid Diet Delights
Liver Health Diet Delights
Low-Calorie Diet Delights
Low-Carb Diet Delights
Low-Fat Diet Delights
Low-Sodium Diet Delights
Low-Sugar Diet Delights
Lymphoma Health Support
  Diet Delights
Multiple Sclerosis Healthy
  Diet Delights
No Flour No Sugar Diet Delights
Organic Food Delights

pH-Friendly Diet Delights
Pregnancy Diet Delights
Raw Food Diet Delights
Sjögren's Syndrome Diet Delights
Soft Food Diet Delights
Thyroid Health Diet Delights

HOLIDAY DELIGHTS
Christmas Delights
Easter Delights
Father's Day Delights
Fourth of July Delights
Grandparent's Day Delights
Halloween Delights
Hanukkah Delights
Labor Day Weekend Delights
Memorial Day Weekend Delights
Mother's Day Delights
New Year's Delights
St. Patrick's Day Delights
Thanksgiving Delights
Valentine Delights

HOOD AND MATSKO
FAMILY FAVORITES
Hood and Matsko Family
  Appetizers Cookbook
Hood and Matsko Family
  Beverages Cookbook
Hood and Matsko Family
  Breads and Rolls Cookbook
Hood and Matsko Family
  Breakfasts Cookbook
Hood and Matsko Family
  Cakes Cookbook
Hood and Matsko Family
  Candies Cookbook
Hood and Matsko Family
  Casseroles Cookbook
Hood and Matsko Family
  Cookies Cookbook
Hood and Matsko Family
  Desserts Cookbook
Hood and Matsko Family

Dressings, Sauces, and
  Condiments Cookbook
Hood and Matsko Family
  Ethnic Cookbook
Hood and Matsko Family
  Jams, Jellies, Syrups,
  Preserves, and Conserves
Hood and Matsko Family
  Main Dishes Cookbook
Hood and Matsko Family,
  Pies Cookbook
Hood and Matsko Family
  Preserving Cookbook
Hood and Matsko Family
  Salads and Salad Dressings
Hood and Matsko Family
  Side Dishes Cookbook
Hood and Matsko Family
  Vegetable Cookbook
Hood and Matsko Family,
  Aunt Katherine's Recipe
  Collection, Vol. I-II
Hood and Matsko Family,
  Grandma Bert's Recipe
  Collection, Vol. I-IV

HOOD AND MATSKO
FAMILY HOLIDAY
Hood and Matsko Family
  Favorite Birthday Recipes
Hood and Matsko Family
  Favorite Christmas Recipes
Hood and Matsko Family
  Favorite Christmas Sweets
Hood and Matsko Family
  Easter Cookbook
Hood and Matsko Family
  Favorite Thanksgiving Recipes

INTERNATIONAL
DELIGHTS
African Delights
African American Delights
Australian Delights

Austrian Delights
Brazilian Delights
Canadian Delights
Chilean Delights
Chinese Delights
Czechoslovakian Delights
English Delights
Ethiopian Delights
Fijian Delights
French Delights
German Delights
Greek Delights
Hungarian Delights
Icelandic Delights
Indian Delights
Irish Delights
Italian Delights
Korean Delights
Kosovo Delights
Macedonia Republic Delights
Mexican Delights
Montenegro Delights
Native American Delights
Polish Delights
Russian Delights
Scottish Delights
Serbian Delights
Slovakian Delights
Slovenian Delights
Sri Lanka Delights
Swedish Delights
Thai Delights
The Netherlands Delights
Yugoslavian Delights
Zambian Delights

REGIONAL DELIGHTS
Glacier National Park Delights
Northwest Regional Delights
Oregon Coast Delights
Schweitzer Mountain Delights
Southwest Regional Delights
Tropical Delights

Washington Wine Country
  Delights
Wine Delights of Walla
  Walla Wineries
Yellowstone National Park Delights

SEASONAL DELIGHTS
Autumn Harvest Delights
Spring Harvest Delights
Summer Harvest Delights
Winter Harvest Delights

SPECIAL EVENTS DELIGHTS
Birthday Delights
Coffee Klatch Delights
Super Bowl Delights
Tea Time Delights

STATE DELIGHTS
Alaska Delights
Arizona Delights
Georgia Delights
Hawaii Delights
Idaho Delights
Illinois Delights
Iowa Delights
Louisiana Delights
Minnesota Delights
Montana Delights
North Dakota Delights
Oregon Delights
South Dakota Delights
Texas Delights
Washington Delights

U.S. TERRITORIES DELIGHTS
Cruzan Delights
U.S. Virgin Island Delights

MISCELLANEOUS COOKBOOKS
Getaway Studio Cookbook
The Soup Doctor's Cookbook

BILINGUAL DELIGHTS SERIES

Apple Delights, English-French Edition
Apple Delights, English-Russian Edition
Apple Delights, English-Spanish Edition
Huckleberry Delights, English-French Edition
Huckleberry Delights, English-Russian Edition
Huckleberry Delights, English-Spanish Edition

CATHOLIC DELIGHTS SERIES

Apple Delights Catholic
Coffee Delights Catholic
Easter Delights Catholic
Huckleberry Delights Catholic
Tea Delights Catholic

CATHOLIC BILINGUAL DELIGHTS SERIES

Apple Delights Catholic, English-French Edition
Apple Delights Catholic, English-Russian Edition
Apple Delights Catholic, English-Spanish Edition

Huckleberry Delights Catholic, English-Spanish Edition

CHRISTIAN DELIGHTS SERIES

Apple Delights Christian
Coffee Delights Christian
Easter Delights Christian
Huckleberry Delights Christian
Tea Delights Christian

CHRISTIAN BILINGUAL DELIGHTS SERIES

Apple Delights Christian, English-French Edition
Apple Delights Christian, English-Russian Edition
Apple Delights Christian, English-Spanish Edition
Huckleberry Delights Christian, English-Spanish Edition

FUNDRAISING COOKBOOKS

Ask about our fundraising cookbooks to help raise funds for your organization.

The above books are also available in bilingual versions. Please contact Whispering Pine Press International, Inc., for details.

The above list of books is not all-inclusive. For a complete list please visit our website or contact us at:

Whispering Pine Press International, Inc.
Your Northwest Book Publishing Company
P.O. Box 214
Spokane Valley, WA 99037-0214 USA
Phone: (509) 928-8700 | Fax: (509) 922-9949
Email: sales@WhisperingPinePress.com
Publisher Websites: www.WhisperingPinePress.com
www.WhisperingPinePressBookstore.com
Blog: www.WhisperingPinePressBlog.com

Blueberry Delights Cookbook

A Collection of Blueberry Recipes
Cookbook Delights Series-Book 2

Karen Jean Matsko Hood

Published by:

Whispering Pine Press International, Inc.
Your Northwest Book Publishing Company
P.O. Box 214
Spokane Valley, WA 99037-0214 USA
Phone: (509) 928-8700 | Fax: (509) 922-9949
Email: sales@WhisperingPinePress.com
Websites: www.WhisperingPinePress.com
www.WhisperingPinePressBookStore.com
Blog: www.WhisperingPinePressBlog.com
SAN 253-200X
Printed in the U.S.A.

Published by Whispering Pine Press International, Inc.
P.O. Box 214
Spokane Valley, Washington 99037-0214 USA

For sales outside the United States, please contact the Whispering Pine Press International, Inc., International Sales Department.

Manufactured in the United States of America. This paper is acid-free and 100% chlorine free.

Book and Cover Design by Artistic Design Service, Inc.
P. O. Box 1792
Spokane Valley, WA 99037-1792 USA
www.ArtisticDesignService.com

Library of Congress Number (LCCN): 2014901411

Hood, Karen Jean Matsko
    Title: Blueberry Delights Cookbook: A Collection of Blueberry Recipes: Cookbook Delights Series-Book 2

        p.   cm.

ISBN: 978-1-59434-049-9   case bound
ISBN: 978-1-59649-455-8   perfect bound
ISBN: 978-1-59649-456-5   spiral bound
ISBN: 978-1-59210-775-9   comb bound
ISBN: 978-1-59210-776-6   E-PDF
ISBN: 978-1-59210-346-1   E-PUB
ISBN: 978-1-59649-457-2   E-PRC

First Edition: February 2014
1. Cookery *(Blueberry Delights Cookbook: A Collection of Blueberry Recipes: Cookbook Delights Series-Book 2)*   1. Title

Blueberry Delights Cookbook

A Collection of Blueberry Recipes
Cookbook Delights Series-Book 2

Gift Inscription

To: _____

_____

From: _____

_____

Date: _____

_____

Special Message: _____

_____

_____

_____

_____

_____

_____

_____

_____

*It is always nice to receive a personal note to
create a special memory.*

www.BlueberryDelightsCookbook.com
www.WhisperingPinePress.com
www.WhisperingPinePressBookstore.com

Dedications

To my husband and best friend, Jim.

To our seventeen children: Gabriel, Brianne Kristina and her husband Moulik Kothari, Marissa Kimberly, Janelle Karina and her husband Paul Turcotte, Mikayla Karlene, Kyler James, Kelsey Katrina, Corbin Joel, Caleb Jerome, Keisha Kalani Hiwot, Devontay Joshua, Kianna Karielle Selam, Rosy Kiara, Mercedes Katherine, Jasmine Khalia Wengel, Cheyenne Krystal, and Annalise Kaylee Marie.

To our grandchild Nola Paige and our future grandchildren.

To our foster grandchild, Courtney, Lorenzo, and Leah.

To my brother, Stephen, and his wife, Karen.

To my husband's ten siblings: Gary, Colleen, John, Dan, Mary, Ray, Ann, Teresa, Barbara, Agnes, and their families.

In loving memory of my mom, who passed away in 2007; my dad, who passed away in 1976; and my sister, Sandy, who passed away due to multiple sclerosis in 1999.

To Sandy's three sons: Monte, Bradley, and Derek. To Monte's wife, Sarah, and their children: Liam, Alice, Charlie, and Samuel and their foster children. To Bradley's wife, Shawnda, and their children: Anton, Isaac, and Isabel.

To our foster children past and present: Krystal, Sara, Rebecca, Janice, Devontay Joshua, Mercedes Katherine, Zha'Nell, Makia, Onna, Cheyenne Krystal, Onna Marie, Nevaeh, and Zada, our future foster children, and all foster children everywhere.

To the Court Appointed Special Advocate (CASA) Volunteer Program in the judicial system which benefits abused and neglected children.

To the Literacy Campaign dedicated to promoting literacy throughout the world.

Acknowledgements

The author would like to acknowledge all those individuals who helped me during my time in writing this book. Appreciation is extended for all their support and effort they put into this project.

Deep gratitude and profound thanks are owed to my husband, Jim, for giving freely of his time and encouragement during this project.

Thanks are owed to my children Gabriel, Brianne Kristina and her husband Moulik Kothari, Marissa Kimberly, Janelle Karina and her husband Paul Turcotte, Mikayla Karlene, Kyler James, Kelsey Katrina, Corbin Joel, Caleb Jerome, Keisha Kalani Hiwot, Devontay Joshua, Kianna Karielle Selam, Rosy Kiara, Mercedes Katherine, Jasmine Khalia Wengel, Cheyenne Krystal, and Annalise Kaylee Marie. All of these persons inspire my writing.

Thanks are due to Teresa L. Allen and Sharron Thompson for their assistance in typing and editing this manuscript for publication. Thanks go to Artistic Design Service, Inc. for their assistance in formatting and providing a graphic design of this manuscript for publication. This project could not have been completed without them.

Many thanks are due to members of my family, all of whom were very supportive during the time it took to complete this project. Their patience and support are greatly appreciated.

Blueberry Delights Cookbook

Table of Contents

Blueberry Delights Cookbook

A Collection of Blueberry Recipes
Cookbook Delights Series-Book 2

Introduction

Blueberries are a beautiful blue-purple berry native to the eastern half of the United States, but they are now grown extensively throughout the East, Midwest, and West. A close relative of huckleberries, blueberries have a mellow, delicious flavor unlike any other berry.

Blueberries have an interesting history of facts and folklore. Their blossoms are bell-shaped and beautiful, and the fruit is delicious to eat cooked or raw. It is no wonder that blueberry bush cultivation spread quickly throughout the United States.

Some of this blueberry folklore is included in this book. As a poet, I found it enjoyable to color this cookbook with poetry so that the reader can savor the metaphorical richness of the blueberry, as well as its literal flavor. Also included in this cookbook are some articles on history, folklore, cultivation and botanical information, along with interesting facts about blueberries.

The *Cookbook Delights Series* would not be complete without *Blueberry Delights Cookbook,* because blueberries are a delicious and popular American fruit. We hope you enjoy reading it as well as trying out all of the recipes. This cookbook is designed for easy use and is organized into alphabetical sections: appetizers and dips; beverages; breads and rolls; breakfasts; cakes; candies; cookies; desserts; dressings, sauces, and condiments; jams, jellies, and syrups; main dishes; pies; preserving; salads; side dishes; soups; and wines and spirits.

Do enjoy your reading about blueberries, but most importantly, have fun with those you care about while you are cooking.

Following is a collection of recipes gathered and modified to bring you *Blueberry Delights Cookbook: A Collection of Blueberry Recipes, Cookbook Delights Series* by Karen Jean Matsko Hood.

Blueberry Delights Cookbook
A Collection of Blueberry Recipes
Cookbook Delights Series-Book 2

Blueberry Botanical Classification

Blueberry Botanical Classification

Scientific Name	Common Name	Main Features
Vaccinium corymbosum	Northern Highbush Blueberry	Flower ⅜ inch long, white to pale pink petals.
Vaccinium "Berkeley"	Northern Blueberry	Bright yellow wood in the winter, powder blue fruit in late midseason.
Vaccinium Bluecrop	Northern Blueberry	Upright, open-growing shrub to 5 to 6 feet, attractive shades of red in fall.
Vaccinium Bluejay	Northern Blueberry	Early midseason, 6 to 7 feet with light green summer foliage, yellow-orange leaves in fall, and bright yellow wood in winter.
Vaccinium Brigitta	Northern Blueberry	Late season; amazing shelf life of over 30 days when refrigerated; fruit is large, light blue, firm with crisp texture, and sweet yet very slightly tart.
Vaccinium Olympia	Northern Blueberry	Midseason, pleasant aroma and spicy flavor, perfect for muffins and pancakes. Avoid growing in areas with late spring frosts, as it can be susceptible.
Vaccinium Chandler	Northern Blueberry	Fruit the size of cherries, world's largest blueberry, long ripening season yields fresh fruit for over 6 weeks.
Vaccinium Chippewa	Northern Blueberry	Light blue berries with excellent sweet flavor, yields 3½ to 7 pounds per bush at maturity.
Vaccinium Duke	Northern Blueberry	Early producer; berries the size of quarters with tangy, delicious, sweet flavor; blooms late and ripens early.

Blueberry Delights Cookbook

A Collection of Blueberry Recipes
Cookbook Delights Series-Book 2

Blueberry Cultivation and Gardening

Blueberry Cultivation and Gardening

Blueberries require a soil pH of 4.0 to 5.5. If azaleas and rhododendrons flourish in your garden, blueberries will, too. It is beneficial to test your soil's pH level. If the soil is over 6.2 on the pH scale, you should grow your blueberries on mounded beds of amended soil or in containers. If your soil is in the 5.3 to 6.0 range, amending the soil will usually work. Mixing an acidic material into the soil will lower its pH. Peat moss was normally used, but taking this material destroys the ecology of peat bogs. It is best to use composted leaves, pine or hemlock needles, oak, beech, and chestnut leaves and/or bark, hardwood and softwood sawdust, or bald-cypress leaves and composted cypress bark. To counteract this deficiency, add cottonseed or blood meal, dry manure, or packaged high-nitrogen fertilizers. Make sure to check the moisture in amended soil. If the peat, sawdust, or other finely ground materials dry out, they will repel rainwater instead of soaking it up.

Blueberries have shallow roots; therefore, when amending the soil, you need not dig too deeply – about 8 inches is sufficient. Your soil should end up light, loose, crumbly, and moisture retentive (but well drained), like the sandy, humus-like, woodland soil in which they naturally grow.

Blueberries should be grown in a sunny location. Avoid planting them in "frost pockets," where cold air settles, such as at the bottom of a hill or other low-lying area. When transplanting them, do not let the roots freeze or dry out and do not expose them to sunlight, which will kill the small, fibrous roots. Protect the bare roots with a damp, lightproof covering.

Highbush varieties should be planted 3 feet apart if a formal hedge is desired. If you want a natural setting, plant them 4 to 6 feet apart. Rabbiteye varieties should be grown up to 8 feet apart or closer for a hedge. Lowbush varieties can be grown 2 to 3 feet apart or 1 to 2 feet apart for a ground cover. Since blueberries have shallow roots that can easily be damaged by drought, tilling, hoeing, and even handpicking weeds, it is wise to use mulch (as mentioned before) to prevent weeds and retain moisture. When checking to make sure the soil is moist, push away a bit of mulch and stick your finger into the soil.

Container-growing blueberries: Blueberries can easily be grown in containers if your soil pH is beyond simple repair or if space is limited. They will flourish if kept well watered and fed regularly with high-nitrogen fertilizer.

A good soil mix for blueberries is made by combining two parts garden soil, one part compost, two parts composted chopped leaves or peat, and two parts coarse builders sand. If you garden in a cold-winter climate, bring the containers into an unheated garage or porch for the winter. Mulch the roots with a thick layer of leaves, and wrap the plant in burlap for extra protection in extreme temperatures. Be sure to water them during the winter months whenever needed; do not let the soil become bone dry.

Fertilizer: If your soil needed no amendments to correct the pH, each spring the mulch around each plant should be pulled back and ½ to 1 pound of high-nitrogen fertilizer, such as dry manure, cottonseed or soybean meal, or a high-nitrogen packaged organic fertilizer, should be applied. Fertilizer formulated for rhododendrons and azaleas can be used for blueberries, although a little less fertilizer than the recommended amount should be used. Keep an eye on the plants for signs of nitrogen deficiency. If the foliage turns yellow and then red, when it should be green, a nitrogen deficiency is probably the cause. Correct this immediately by adding a high-nitrogen liquid fertilizer along with a fast-acting foliar spray to the plants showing stress.

Pruning: Blueberries are easily maintained, as they naturally grow in a neat shape. Sometimes, a harsh winter will kill off some or even all of a blueberry's branches; cut off these damaged branches at an outward-facing node where healthy wood begins. As blueberries age, the canes become less productive and their tips twiggy. Cut back the twiggy ends of the older branches, and thin out six-year-old and older canes once in a while to make room for younger, more productive canes.

Harvesting: Most blueberries begin to produce fruit at age three, which is the first year in your garden if you planted 3-year-old bushes, and can continue to bear for up to 40 years. Depending on the type and variety of your plants and on your growing area, blueberries ripen from mid to late summer over a period of two weeks or longer. The berries do not ripen all at one time. The "bluecrop" season lasts a month. Turning blue is a sign of ripening, not a sign of ripeness. Most blueberries turn blue one to two weeks before they are ready to pick. Ripe berries will twist off the stems easily. A taste test is another way to tell if harvest time has arrived.

Pests and Diseases: Home gardeners have little trouble from pests. Two types of insect larvae, the cherry fruit worm and the blueberry maggot, are occasionally troublesome. Diseases are also rare in the home garden but can sometimes cause problems in warm, humid areas, such as the South. Birds will be your worst enemy when it comes to protecting your crop. Thrushes and other songbirds will be the most problematic. Some people resort to building a permanent cage for their blueberries, but plastic mesh bird netting works just as well. Drape it over the bush, making sure there are no gaps or openings, and secure it to the base of the canes. If birds reach through the mesh, suspend it on a frame a foot or so above the berries. The berries are also eaten by bears and small mammals. Deer and rabbits browse on the twigs and leaves as well. If animals become especially troublesome, a fence or cage is the best solution.

Propagation: Blueberries are usually propagated from hardwood cuttings, but the process is difficult. It is better to purchase plants from nurseries. If your local nursery does not provide blueberry cuttings, you can purchase them via several mail-order catalogs.

Blueberry Delights Cookbook

A Collection of Blueberry Recipes
Cookbook Delights Series-Book 2

Blueberry Facts

Blueberry Facts

The blueberry is native to northern North America. Native Americans ate blueberries fresh and also dried them for later use. They used them in stews and soups, as well as in a pudding along with cornmeal.

Blueberries are one of the most popular of the berries. They are simply delicious and ever-so-versatile. They can be eaten fresh or baked into pies, muffins, and other treats. Blueberries can be dried, canned, or frozen for use throughout the winter. These vigorous growing plants, which do not require severe pruning, are quite resistant to pests and diseases. The only thing these plants are very particular about is the soil's pH, which should be around 4.0 to 5.5.

Blueberries are attractive landscape plants with their bell-shaped, waxy, white flowers in the spring and vivid autumn foliage. They can be pruned to have a tree shape or a low hedge shape.

There are three main types of blueberries: lowbush, highbush, and rabbiteye. A variety of hybrids have been developed that can survive the bitter cold winters of the North and withstand the extreme heat of the South. There are high-growing varieties, which can make a pleasant, natural fence between properties and low-growing varieties for people with limited spaces. Blueberries are self-pollinating, but if you cross-pollinate with another plant, the fruit will be larger, ripen earlier, and have fewer seeds. Blueberries begin to ripen in early summer and continue over a period of several weeks.

In the United States, New Jersey raises the most cultivated fresh blueberries. Michigan grows more berries, but two-thirds of its crop goes for processing. Maine produces only wild blueberries, and much of its crop is processed by freezing. In Nova Scotia, Canada, wild blueberries are the most important fruit crop commercially, producing 30 million pounds of wild berries each year.

Blueberry Delights Cookbook

A Collection of Blueberry Recipes
Cookbook Delights Series-Book 2

Blueberry Folklore

Blueberry Folklore

The Northeast Native American tribes revered blueberries, and much folklore developed around them. The blossom end of each berry, the calyx, forms the shape of a perfect five-pointed star; the elders of the tribe would tell of how the Great Spirit sent "star berries" to relieve the children's hunger during a famine. Parts of the blueberry plant were also used as medicine. A tea made from the leaves of the plant was thought to be good for the blood. Blueberry juice was used to treat coughs.

The juice also made an excellent dye for baskets and cloth. In food preparation, dried blueberries were added to stews, soups, and meats. The dried berries were also crushed into a powder and rubbed into meat for flavor. Blueberries were also used for medicinal purposes along with the leaves and roots. A beef jerky called *Sautauthig (pronounced saw'-taw-teeg)*, was made with dried blueberries and meat and was consumed year round.

During the seventeenth century, settlers from England arrived in the New World to begin colonies. The land and the climate were far different from what they left behind, and many early attempts at farming failed.

In the winter of 1620, the Pilgrims established a settlement at Plymouth. Many settlers died during the first few months, but those that survived went on to build homes and establish farms. Their neighbors, the Wampanoag Indians, taught the settlers new skills that helped them survive. They showed them how to plant corn and how to gather and use native plants to supplement their food supply. One important native crop was blueberries the colonists learned from Native Americans how to gather blueberries, dry them under the summer's sun, and store them for the winter.

Blueberry Delights Cookbook
A Collection of Blueberry Recipes
Cookbook Delights Series-Book 2

Blueberry History

Blueberry History

Little is known of the blueberry's early history. For centuries, blueberries were gathered from the forests and the bogs by Native Americans and consumed fresh and also preserved. The first settlers learned how to harvest and preserve the blueberry from the Native Americans. In time, blueberries became an important food source and were preserved and later canned. A beverage made with blueberries was an important staple for Civil War Soldiers. In the 1880s a blueberry canning industry began in the Northeast U.S.A.

Blueberries, also known as bilberries, whortleberries, and hurtleberries, are named for their velvety, deep-blue color, of course. The shrub is of the genus *Vaccinium*, from the Latin *vacca* for cow since cows love them, a fact first noted by Captain James Cook in the late 1700s. They are often confused with huckleberries, which are of the *Gaylussacia* genus. Blueberries used to be picked by hand until the invention of the blueberry rake by Abijah Tabbutt of Maine in 1822, so it is no wonder that Maine's state berry is the blueberry.

The most popular variety is *Vaccinium corymbosum*, known as the "highbush" blueberry. The wild "lowbush" varieties are a favorite of those who like to pick their own in the wilds.

In the early 1900s Elizabeth White and Dr. Frederick Coville worked to domesticate the wild highbush blueberry. Over the decades others have worked to enhance the most desirable qualities of the various highbush blueberries to produce a superior blueberry that is plump, with a deep, rich color and a fruity flavor.

The blueberry industry has grown over the years to include more that 38 states and provinces of Canada, as well as South America, Australia, New Zealand, and Europe.

Blueberry Delights Cookbook
A Collection of Blueberry Recipes
Cookbook Delights Series-Book 2

Blueberry Nutrition and Health

Blueberry Nutrition and Health

Blueberries are a great choice to add to your diet because they not only taste great but have great health and nutritional benefits as well.

Blueberries were prominent in Russian folk medicine as a preventative measure and cure for abdominal problems. The blueberry is still prized for its antioxidant health benefits and as a laxative, as well as other folk remedies. During World War II, British Royal Air Force pilots consumed bilberries (a blueberry relative), which purportedly improved their night vision. Later studies showed a sound basis for this practice. Blueberries are also high in iron.

Researchers at the USDA Human Nutrition Center (HNRCA) have found that blueberries rank number 1 in antioxidant activity when compared to 40 other fresh fruits and vegetables. Antioxidants help neutralize harmful by-products of metabolism called "free radicals" that can lead to cancer and other age-related diseases. Anthocyanin, the pigment that makes the blueberries blue, is thought to be responsible for this major health benefit. This is great news for blueberry lovers.

In another USDA HNRCA lab, neuroscientists discovered that feeding blueberries to laboratory rats slowed age-related loss in their mental capacity, a finding that has important implications for humans. Again, the high antioxidant activity of blueberries probably played a role.

Blueberries may reduce the buildup of so-called "bad" cholesterol that contributes to cardiovascular disease and stroke, according to scientists at the University of California at Davis. Antioxidants are believed to be the active component.

Researchers at Rutgers University in New Jersey have identified a compound in blueberries that promotes urinary tract health and reduces the risk of infection. It appears to work by preventing bacteria from adhering to the cells that line the walls of the urinary tract.

Today, blueberries are being studied in health and medicinal studies. Eating blueberries may help you stay healthier, longer. And that is delicious news indeed.

Blueberry Delights Cookbook

A Collection of Blueberry Recipes
Cookbook Delights Series-Book 2

Poetry

A Collection of Poetry with Blueberry Themes

Table of Contents

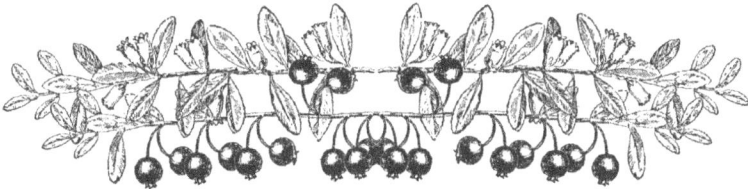

Blueberries Blue

Blueberry leaves blow across windswept landscape
Lovely luscious fruit
Under the branches of the blueberry bush
Earthly treasures of bountiful feasts
Blueberries, blueberries, blueberries, blue
Every berry bursts with flavor
Rushing to pluck them
Red paints the leaves once green every fall
Into pies, desserts, and ice cream they go
Eat them all!
Succulent berries of blueberry delight.

Karen Jean Matsko Hood ©2014
Published in *Blueberry Delights Cookbook*, 2014
By Whispering Pine Press International, Inc., 2014

Blueberry Ice

Cool, refreshing, sweet, yet tart
cold blue, blueberry ice.

From shrub to basket
basket to table

so many recipes
so many peculations.

Be it dessert or pie,
ice cream or sorbet

All will delight
in the blueberry fruit.
Cool blue flavor of
blueberry ice.

Karen Jean Matsko Hood ©2014
Published in *Blueberry Delights Cookbook*, 2014
By Whispering Pine Press International, Inc., 2014

Blueberry Memories

Lush, blueberry ice cream drips blue cream,
blueberry textures, pile high and
perch upon homemade cones.
Children taste their favorite while grandparents wait.
Blueberry candy twists and
spirals on blueberry mounds that punctuate tiny ice
crystals.
Delicious blue memories, the royal
display of colors, fragrant in
our childhood minds to
make many fond memories.

Karen Jean Matsko Hood ©2014
Published in *Blueberry Delights Cookbook*, 2014
By Whispering Pine Press International, Inc., 2014

Blueberry Blossoms

Blueberries blossom with
> Telegrams of love that flourish,
> Elegant calligraphy expressed by each petal
> Reminds me of the man I love.

Each spring my beloved gets so excited
> To watch the blueberries ripen
> Like suspended white ornaments
> On emerging hills of green.

White blossoms replace the withering snow and
> Trade ice for the warmth of spring.
> Lacy blossoms peek out from twigs,
> Rainy cold still looms.

Daffodils smile their friendly greeting,
> And hummingbirds return.
> Down the road the rhubarb sprouts.
> Hyacinths perfume their song.

Muddy fields wait to dry
> As gardeners select their seed.
> Blueberries blossom on the hillsides,
> Upland fields adorned with splotches of white;

> Spring communiqué to my love.

Karen Jean Matsko Hood ©2014
Published in *Blueberry Delights Cookbook*, 2014
By Whispering Pine Press International, Inc., 2014

Blueberry Cluster

Shrubs of similar roots,
similar yet different,
sway in the wind
now still.
Exclamations of leaves gather
in one spot.

There, in the branches of cover,
Gold spheres of blue
decorate the leaves,
now turning shades of amber and gold.

From the north,
blows cool winds.
From the south,
walk humans
both in search of royal treasure.
Rocks grumble, branches snap.
Can nature harmonize
in the sunset?
    For one moment . . .
    nothing changes.

Karen Jean Matsko Hood ©2014
Published in *Blueberry Delights Cookbook*, 2014
By Whispering Pine Press International, Inc., 2014

Blueberry Petals

White petals unfold to reveal
blue-purple berries in bunches.
Visitors pick clusters perched on branches
on decorative branches.
Some look over their shoulder
and invade the space of the secret berry gardens
to search for bountiful, juicy blueberries.

From heavy branches, they pick with wrinkled hands
and seek out each succulent berry.
One by one they fill their buckets
to the top. The fruit line
never seems to reach the rim as
they dip and taste each savory drop
faster than tired hands can fill,
Sweet blue treats,
all from white petals.

Karen Jean Matsko Hood ©2014
Published in *Blueberry Delights Cookbook*, 2014
By Whispering Pine Press International, Inc., 2014

Motherly Gardening

My mother
Taught me
To garden
To dig with bare hands
In clay and
Loam,
And crawl with
Montana angleworms,
That shine in dim
Rays that reflect
From Big
Sky. My mind
Wanders
Through the muck,
Reddish heavy,
Muddy ooze.
Intrigued with
Life
And worms,
Those bugs
Slink through
The gumbo,
Slip
In its
Heaviness.
Great Falls' wind
Reminds
Me to
Plant those
Seeds
Before Chinook
Winds come
To make
More mud.
Wise old mom
Knew that
Earthen mire
Grounded me
In ways
Earthworms
Inch and
Always
Understand.

Karen Jean Matsko Hood ©2014
Published in *Blueberry Delights Cookbook*, 2014
By Whispering Pine Press International, Inc., 2014

Bluebird Beckons

The bluebird beckons me
Down the trail
To follow this first-prize ribbon.
Staccato waves,
    I watch;
Gentle breeze,
    I feel.

Flutter and frolic,
The bluebird sings
And motions me once again
Further down the path.
    I wander,
To watch the fleeing royals.
    I see.

All is still.
Fragrance of bright
Spring blossoms
    I smell.

Deeply fill my cup.
    I drink.
Saturate my skin,
    I taste.

Alas, the moment is broken
With the scolding of the wren.
A step in the rhythm of time
    I hear.

    Listen.

Karen Jean Matsko Hood ©2014
Published in *Blueberry Delights Cookbook*, 2014
By Whispering Pine Press International, Inc., 2014

Blue

Glacier park is separate
in wilderness
not understood by the hands
of a clock antique.

Still true glaciers stand
before final death rings
when all ice melts
to stay in forms no more.

The thought that these ancient
monoliths will exist no more
like the death of a grandparent
not shared by children
obscures beauty as we know it.

The thought that we are
a mere speck of no significance
in the scale of our galaxy
confuses our thoughts
as we know them.

Karen Jean Matsko Hood ©2014
Published in *Blueberry Delights Cookbook*, 2014
By Whispering Pine Press International, Inc., 2014

Blueberry Delights Cookbook
A Collection of Blueberry Recipes
Cookbook Delights Series-Book 2

Blueberry Types

Blueberry Types

True wild blueberries (section *Cyanococcus* of the genus *Vaccinium*) occur only in eastern North America. Other sections in the genus, native to other parts of the world including western North America, Europe, and Asia, include other wild shrubs producing similar-looking edible berries such as huckleberries, cranberries, bilberries, and cowberries.

Northern Highbush Blueberry (*V. corymbosum*) is a species of blueberry native to eastern North America, growing from Nova Scotia and Ontario south to Alabama and west to Wisconsin.

It is a deciduous shrub growing 6 to 12 feet tall, often found in dense thickets. The dark, glossy green leaves are elliptical and 1 to 3½ inches long. The flowers are white, bell-shaped, about ½ inch long. The fruit is a dark blue to black berry ¼ to ½ inches in diameter. This plant grows best in wooded or open areas with moist, acidic soils.

The Northern Highbush Blueberry is the most common commercially-grown blueberry in North America.

Lowbush Blueberry (*V. angustifolium*) is a species of blueberry native to eastern and central Canada and the northeastern United States, growing as far south as West Virginia and west to Minnesota and Manitoba.

It is a low-spreading, deciduous shrub growing to 18 to 24 inches tall. The leaves are glossy blue-green in summer, turning purple in the fall. The leaf shape is broad to elyptic. Buds are brownish red in stem axels. The flowers are white, bell-shaped, ¼ inch long.

The fruit is a small, sweet dark blue to black berry. This plant grows best in wooded or open areas with well-drained acidic soils. In some areas it produces natural blueberry barrens, where it is practically the only species covering large areas.

The plant is fire-tolerant and its numbers often increase in an area following a forest fire.

This native plant is also grown commercially in Canada and Maine, mainly harvested from managed wild patches. It is also a favorite of recreational berry pickers, black bears, rodents, and birds.

Darrow's Blueberry, Evergreen Blueberry, or Southern Highbush Blueberry (*V. darrowii*) is a species of *Vaccinium* in the blueberry group (*Vaccinium* sect. *Cyanococcus*). It is native to the southeastern United States, in Alabama, Florida, Georgia, Louisiana, and Mississippi.

It is an evergreen shrub growing 1 to 4 feet tall, with small, simple ovoid-acute leaves about ½ inch long. The flowers are white, bell-shaped, about ¼ inch long. The fruit is a berry about ¼ inch in diameter, blue-black with a whitish waxy bloom.

There are several different varieties with different ripening times ranging from very early season to late season.

Rabbiteye Blueberry (*V. virgatum*, also known as *V. ashei*) is a species of blueberry native to the southeastern United States, from North Carolina south to Florida and west to Texas. Other common names include Southern Highbush Blueberry, Southern Black Blueberry, and Smallflower Blueberry.

It is a deciduous shrub growing to 15 feet tall, though usually less, commonly only 4 to 6 feet tall. The leaves are spirally arranged, oblanceolate to narrow elliptic, 1¼ to 2 inches long. The flowers are white, bell-shaped, about ¼ inch long. The fruit is a berry ¼ inch in diameter, dark blue to black, bloomed pale blue-gray by a thin wax coating. It grows best in acid soil and is subject to few pests and diseases.

Rabbiteye blueberries are self-infertile and must have two or more varieties to pollinate each other. Honeybees are inefficient pollinators, and carpenter bees frequently cut the corollas to rob nectar without pollinating the flowers. Rabbiteyes do best when pollinated by buzz pollination by bees, such as the native southeastern blueberry bee, *Habropoda laboriosa*.

The species is cultivated for its edible berries, which are similar to other blueberries. It is also grown as an ornamental plant for its fall colors, typically bright orange or red.

Canadian Blueberry (*V. myrtilloides*) is a species of blueberry native to Canada and the northeastern and northwestern

United States, as well as the Great Lakes states. Other common names are Velvetleaf Blueberry, Common Blueberry, Sourtop Blueberry, and Velvetleaf Huckleberry. It hybridizes in the wild with the Lowbush blueberry (*V. angustifolium*).

It is a low-spreading, deciduous shrub growing to 2 feet tall, often in small thickets. The leaves are bright green, paler underneath with velvety hairs. The flowers are white, bell-shaped, ⅛ to ¼ inch long. The fruit is a small, sweet bright blue to dark blue berry, ¼ to ⅓ inch in diameter. Young stems have stiff, dense, bristly hairs. This plant grows best in open coniferous woods with dry, loose acidic soils; it is also found in forested bogs and rocky areas. It is fire-tolerant and is often abundant following forest fires or clear-cut logging.

This native plant is also grown commercially in Canada and Maine, mainly harvested from managed wild patches. It is one of the sweetest blueberries known. It is also an important food source for black bears, deer, small mammals, and birds.

Elliott's Blueberry (*V. elliottii*) is a species of *Vaccinium* in the blueberry group (*Vaccinium* sect. *Cyanococcus*), commonly called the Mayberry. It is native to the southeastern United States, from southeastern Virginia south to Florida and west to Arkansas and Texas.

It is a deciduous shrub 6 to 12 feet tall, with small, simple ovoid-acute leaves about 1 inch long with a finely serrated margin. The flowers are pale pink, bell-shaped, ¼ inch long, opening in the early spring before the new leaves appear. The fruit is an edible berry ½ inch in diameter, blue-black, only rarely with a whitish waxy bloom; they ripen from late spring (in Florida) through summer. It produces a particularly large yield of somewhat sour berries. It is popular for late-season fruit.

Blueberry Delights Cookbook

A Collection of Blueberry Recipes
Cookbook Delights Series-Book 2

RECIPES

Blueberry Delights Cookbook

A Collection of Blueberry Recipes
Cookbook Delights Series-Book 2

Appetizers and Dips

Table of Contents

Page

Did You Know? . . . .

Did you know that the Rabbit eye Blueberry is also grown as an ornamental plant for its fall colors, typically bright orange or red?

Mixed Berry Pizza

The fresh fruit in this appealing appetizer is a change of pace from the usual dips. The crescent roll crust is started the night before and makes enough for two pizzas (or one pizza and a batch of rolls). If you do not have time to make your crust from scratch, you can use one 8-ounce tube of refrigerated crescent rolls.

Ingredients for crescent roll crust:

  1 pkg. yeast
  3 Tbs. warm water
  ½ c. butter
  1 tsp. salt
  1 c. boiling water
  2 eggs
  ½ c. sugar
  4 c. all-purpose flour, approximately

Ingredients for filling:

  11 oz. cream cheese, softened
  ½ c. apricot preserves
  2 Tbs. confectioners' sugar
  2 c. sliced fresh strawberries
  1 c. fresh blueberries
  1 c. fresh raspberries

Directions for crescent roll crust:

  1. Dissolve yeast in the 3 tablespoons of warm water.
  2. Place butter and salt in glass measuring cup, and add the 1 cup of boiling water, stirring until salt is dissolved and water is lukewarm.
  3. Beat eggs with sugar until well beaten.
  4. Add lukewarm butter mixture and dissolved yeast.

5. Add 2 cups of flour; mix in well, then add remaining flour, mixing well.
6. Add sufficient flour to make"kneadable" dough, and knead lightly until well mixed.
7. Place in bowl, cover, and refrigerate overnight.
8. Note: Instead of refrigerating, you may let dough rise in warm place for 1½ hours, and then proceed with recipe.
9. When ready to use, cut dough in half.
10. Preheat oven to 375 degrees F.
11. Press half of dough onto bottom and 1 inch up sides of 15 x 10 x 1-inch baking pan coated with nonstick spray.
12. Bake for 8 to 10 minutes or until golden; cool completely.
13. Note: Make two pizzas or use second half for rolls, rolling dough into a round ¼ inch thick. Spread with soft butter, cut into 12 pie-shaped wedges, and roll into crescents. Place on parchment-lined baking sheet, let rise until double in size, then bake at 375 degrees F. for 8 to 10 minutes, until golden brown.

Directions for filling:

1. In mixing bowl beat cream cheese until smooth.
2. Beat in preserves and confectioners' sugar; spread over crust.
3. Cover and refrigerate for 1 to 2 hours.
4. Just before serving, arrange berries on top; cut into 20 pieces.

Yields: 20 servings.

Did You Know? . . . .

Did you know that 1 cup of blueberries contains 84 calories?

Warmed Brie with Blueberry Chutney

Our family loves brie cheese, and this is one of our favorite ways to serve it.

Ingredients:

    1   c. blueberries, fresh or frozen
    2   Tbs. chopped onion
    1½ tsp. grated gingerroot
    ¼   c. brown sugar, firmly packed
    2   Tbs. cider vinegar
    1½ tsp. cornstarch
    ⅛   tsp. salt
    1   cinnamon stick
    1   round Brie cheese (8- or 12-inch)

Directions:

1. In saucepan combine all ingredients except brie cheese; mix well.
2. Bring to a boil over medium heat, stirring frequently, and boil 1 minute.
3. Remove cinnamon sticks, cover, and refrigerate at least 30 minutes.
4. Place brie on microwave-safe serving dish.
5. Microwave on high for 2 to 3 minutes or until warm; remove from oven.
6. Top cheese with cold chutney.
7. Serve with crackers or a sliced baguette.

Did You Know? . . . .

Did you know that the Northern Highbush Blueberry is the most common commercially-grown blueberry in North America?

Chocolate Blueberry Cheese Ball

Try this unique appetizer for a change of pace from the traditional cheese ball. This sweet cheese ball is great to serve with hot chocolate or flavored coffee on a chilly day. It is also good spread on toasted bagels.

Ingredients:

> 6 oz. semisweet chocolate chips
> 1 c. pecans
> 8 oz. cream cheese, softened
> ½ c. dried blueberries (recipe page 253)
>   chocolate-flavored or vanilla wafers
>   chocolate or graham crackers
>   your favorite sweetened cookie or cracker

Directions:

1. Process chocolate chips and pecans in blender or food processor until finely ground.
2. Place mixture in airtight plastic bag or container until ready to use. (There will be enough mixture to make several cheese balls.)
3. When ready to make cheese ball, place cream cheese in bowl.
4. Remove ½ cup of ground chocolate/nut mixture from its bag, and mix into cream cheese along with dried blueberries.
5. Shape into ball and wrap in plastic wrap.
6. Refrigerate for 2 or 3 hours or until firm.
7. Serve with chocolate-flavored or vanilla wafers, chocolate or graham crackers, or your favorite sweetened cookie or cracker.

Luscious Fruit Platter

This fruit platter is at its best in the summer when fruit is fresh and plentiful. If paired with angel food cake, this can also be a tasty dessert.

Ingredients:

    8   oz. cream cheese, softened
    ½   c. milk
    2   Tbs. lemon juice
    4   tsp. sugar
    ¼   tsp. salt
    1   med. honeydew, peeled, seeded, cut into wedges
    1½   c. halved fresh strawberries
    1½   c. cubed, seeded watermelon
    1   c. fresh blueberries
    1   med. firm banana, cut into 1-inch pieces
    2   med. ripe peaches, pitted, quartered
         clusters of red and green seedless grapes

Directions:

1. In small mixing bowl, beat cream cheese.
2. Add milk, lemon juice, sugar, and salt; beat until smooth.
3. Transfer to small serving bowl.
4. On large serving platter, arrange honeydew wedges in spoke pattern.
5. Place strawberries, watermelon, blueberries, banana, peaches, and grapes between wedges.
6. Place dip in center; serve immediately.

Yields: 8 to 10 servings fruit; 2 cups dip.

Blueberry Chicken Salsa Torte

This is an impressive appetizer, and making the blueberry salsa yourself or finding it at your specialty grocer will be well worth the effort.

Ingredients:

- 1 Tbs. olive oil
- 1 sm. onion, cut into strips
- 2 cloves garlic, minced
- 3 c. grated zucchini
- ¾ lb. canned white meat chicken, drained, shredded
- 3 c. shredded Monterey Jack cheese
- 3 flour tortillas
- 16 oz. blueberry salsa (recipe page 185)
- sour cream (optional)

Directions:

1. In large skillet heat oil, then add onion and garlic; sauté for 5 minutes.
2. Add zucchini and sauté for another 5 minutes, stirring occasionally.
3. Remove skillet from heat and drain well; stir in drained, shredded chicken; set aside.
4. Preheat oven to 400 degrees F.
5. Spray 10-inch pie plate with cooking spray.
6. Spread half of chicken mixture into it, then sprinkle with half the cheese.
7. Place 1 tortilla on top of cheese layer, then spread on half the salsa and add 1 more tortilla.
8. Spread on remaining half of salsa then remaining half of chicken mixture over tortilla.
9. Top with 1 more tortilla, and sprinkle with remaining half of cheese.
10. Cover with foil and bake for 40 minutes.
11. Remove cover, and bake for an additional 15 minutes.
12. Remove from oven, and let cool for 10 minutes.
13. Cut into 6 or 8 wedges, and serve with small dollops of sour cream if desired.

Yields: 6 to 8 servings.

Warm and Cheesy Fruit Dip

This blend of cheese and fruit creates a wonderful flavor. Although it can be served with crackers, it is especially wonderful served with sliced apples and pears.

Ingredients:

   16 oz. soft-style cream cheese with pineapple, softened
   ¾ lb. Swiss cheese, shredded
   2 c. dried blueberries (recipe page 253)
   2 Tbs. orange juice
   ¼ c. apple juice

Directions:

1. Preheat oven to 375 degrees F.
2. In medium bowl blend cream cheese, Swiss cheese, blueberries, orange juice, and apple juice.
3. Scoop into 9-inch pie pan.
4. Bake until bubbly and lightly browned, about 15 minutes.
5. Remove from oven, and place on large serving platter with crackers or fruits dipped in lemon juice to prevent discoloration.

Sweet Kielbasa for a Crowd

This is a delicious appetizer for a crowd that you can make earlier in the day in your slow cooker. Once it has cooked on high, you can just turn down the heat and let it simmer the rest of the day until needed. Be sure to have a dish of toothpicks handy for eating utensils.

Ingredients:

   4 pkg. fully cooked kielbasa sausages (16 oz. each)
   1 c. blueberry preserves (recipe page 196)
   2 c. jellied cranberry sauce
   1 can crushed pineapple in heavy syrup (20 oz.)

Directions:

1. Preheat oven to 350 degrees F.
2. Cut kielbasa rings into ¼-inch slices.
3. Place sliced kielbasa into 13 x 9 x 2-inch baking dish.
4. In medium bowl stir together blueberry preserves, cranberry sauce, and crushed pineapple in syrup.
5. Pour over kielbasa and stir to coat.
6. Bake for about 1 hour or until sauce thickens.
7. Note: May also be cooked in slow cooker following same directions but allowing additional time for sauce to thicken. Be sure to turn down to low heat once sauce thickens.
8. Serve with crackers or sliced baguette rounds.

Mini Rice Cake Snacks

Have fun dressing up these bite-size rice cakes with this easy spread and colorful fruits.

Ingredients:

3 oz. cream cheese, softened
¼ c. orange marmalade
24 miniature honey-nut or cinnamon-apple rice cakes
2 med. fresh strawberries, sliced
3 Tbs. fresh blueberries
3 Tbs. Mandarin orange segments
3 Tbs. pineapple tidbits

Directions:

1. In small mixing bowl combine cream cheese and marmalade until blended.
2. Spread over rice cakes; top with fruit.

Yields: 2 dozen.

Frosted Blueberries

These little treats are yummy, and they look nice on your buffet table or served alongside sliced cheese and crackers.

Ingredients:

- 2 lb. extra-large blueberries
- 3 oz. blueberry or grape-flavored gelatin mix

Directions:

1. Rinse blueberries in colander and drain off excess water; blot lightly to almost dry.
2. Pour gelatin mix into bowl; add one handful of berries at a time, and roll around until coated.
3. Transfer to attractive serving dish, and refrigerate for 1 hour to allow gelatin to set before serving.

Blueberry Cheese Rollups

These are delightful little pinwheel-type sandwiches or snacks, and even the children like them as a snack. Not only are they tasty, but they are a healthy alternative to empty calories. These snacks can be made up to 3 days in advance and kept tightly wrapped in the refrigerator.

Ingredients:

- 4 oz. cream cheese, room temperature
- 4 oz. Feta cheese, crumbled
- ¼ c. chopped dried blueberries (recipe page 253)
- ⅓ c. finely chopped fresh spinach leaves
- ¼ c. finely chopped pecans
- 2 flour tortillas

Directions:

1. Bring cream cheese to room temperature; blend both cheeses together until creamy.
2. Stir in blueberries, spinach, and pecans.
3. Spread half the mixture on one tortilla; roll tightly and wrap with plastic wrap.
4. Repeat with second tortilla; chill for at least 3 hours.
5. When ready to serve, slice into rounds and place on tray.

Festive Nut Bowl

This is an easy and quick-to-fix snack. You can add your favorite granola cereal or exchange some nuts with dried fruits for variations.

Ingredients:

½ c. macadamia nuts
½ c. salted cashews
½ c. shelled pistachio nuts
½ c. dried blueberries (recipe page 253)
½ c. dried cranberries
½ c. dried cherries

Directions:

1. In large bowl mix together macadamia nuts, cashews, and pistachios.
2. Add dried blueberries, cranberries, and cherries; toss well to mix.
3. Store in sealed bags for up to 1 month.
4. To serve, place in attractive serving bowls with small serving spoons.

Yields: 3 cups.

Antipasto with Prosciutto, Blueberries, and Balsamic Onions

This is a delicious summertime appetizer, perfect for using your freshly picked blueberries. Do not forget to start your preparations the day before you need this dish.

Ingredients:

- 1 Tbs. olive oil
- 2 lg. red onions, peeled, cut in half, thinly sliced
- 3 Tbs. balsamic vinegar, divided
- ½ lb. prosciutto ham, thinly sliced
- 1½ lb. blueberries, washed
- ⅓ lb. Parmesan cheese or Asiago cheese, thinly sliced

Directions:

1. The day before serving, heat olive oil over medium-high heat in large skillet.
2. Add onions, and quickly sauté just until they begin to soften, about 4 minutes.
3. Stir in 2 tablespoons balsamic vinegar, stirring to coat; transfer mixture to bowl, cover, and refrigerate.
4. Two hours before serving remove onions from refrigeration, and stir in remaining vinegar.
5. Roll each slice of prosciutto loosely, and arrange at one end of large platter; pile blueberries in center and onions at other end.
6. Tuck slices of cheese around platter, and serve.

Yields: 4 to 6 servings.

Did You Know? . . . .

Did you know that the lowbush blueberry is the state fruit of Maine?

Fruit-Topped Canapés

Although this recipe uses specific fruits to top these canapés, other fruits as well as vegetables, such as steamed broccoli flowerets, carrot slices, and asparagus pieces may also be used.

Ingredients:

- 8 oz. cream cheese, softened
- 1 tsp. grated orange rind
- 2 Tbs. orange juice
- ½ tsp. ground ginger
- 48 multi-shaped crackers, lightly toasted
- ¼ med. honeydew melon
- 8 fresh strawberries
- 1-2 kiwifruit
- 1½ c. fresh pineapple wedges, drained
- ¾ c. seedless red grapes
- ¾ c. seedless green grapes
- ½ c. Mandarin orange sections, drained
- ½ c. fresh blueberries
- fresh mint leaves

Directions:

1. Beat cream cheese at medium speed of electric mixer until smooth; add orange rind, orange juice, and ground ginger, mixing well.
2. Spoon mixture into decorating bag fitted with tip No. 18, and pipe mixture onto crackers; set aside.
3. Cut fruit into various shapes, and decorate crackers as desired with fruit and mint leaves.

Yields: 4 dozen.

Chinese Blueberry Barbequed Pork

This version has additional spice and flavoring, but it is just as delicious, if not more so, than the traditional barbeque!

Ingredients:

¼ c. soy sauce
1 Tbs. red wine
1 Tbs. brown sugar, firmly packed
2 Tbs. blueberry preserves (recipe page 196)
1 tsp. red food coloring (optional)
1 tsp. blue food coloring (optional)
½ tsp. ground cinnamon
1 green onion, halved
1 clove garlic, minced
2 pork tenderloins (12 oz. each)
    additional blueberry preserves for dipping
    sesame seeds for dipping

Directions:

1. Combine soy sauce, wine, brown sugar, blueberry preserves, food colorings, cinnamon, onion, and garlic in large bowl.
2. Trim all fat from meat, then add meat to mixture in large bowl, turning to coat completely.
3. Cover and refrigerate 1 hour or overnight, turning meat occasionally; reserve marinade.
4. Preheat oven to 350 degrees F.
5. Place meat on wire rack in baking pan; bake for 45 minutes or until no longer pink in center, basting frequently with marinade.
6. Chill cooked meat in refrigerator until room temperature or slightly chilled.
7. Slice diagonally and serve with a dish of melted blueberry preserves and a dish of sesame seeds alongside for dipping.

Blueberry Delights Cookbook

A Collection of Blueberry Recipes
Cookbook Delights Series-Book 2

Beverages

Table of Contents

Page

Blueberry Breakfast Shake

This makes a tasty, colorful, and nutritious shake to be enjoyed at breakfast or anytime.

Ingredients:

    2 c. plain yogurt
    1 c. fresh blueberries
    1 med. ripe banana
    ½ c. orange juice

Directions:

1. Combine yogurt, blueberries, banana, and orange juice in blender.
2. Blend until smooth and frothy.
3. Pour into glasses.

Blueberry Black Soda

This is an easy-to-make, colorful soda to serve on relaxing summer evenings.

Ingredients:

    3 Tbs. blueberry syrup (recipe page 200)
    1 Tbs. blackberry syrup
    1 c. sparkling water or club soda
       ice

Directions:

1. Fill 16-ounce glass or shaker jar about ¾ full with ice; add both syrups and sparkling water or soda.
2. Stir or shake and serve.

Yields: 1 serving.

Blueberry Fruit Smoothie

This smoothie is a nutritious alternative to traditional malts, shakes, and sodas. A reduced fat version can be made by using low-fat ice cream and yogurt.

Ingredients:

  1 c. vanilla ice cream
  1 c. blueberries, fresh or frozen
  ½ c. chopped peaches, fresh or frozen, thawed
  ½ c. pineapple juice
  ¼ c. vanilla yogurt

Directions:

  1. In blender combine all ingredients; cover and process until smooth.
  2. Pour into chilled glasses; serve immediately.

Yields: 3 servings.

Wild Blueberry Smoothie

This smoothie is easy to make and very refreshing.

Ingredients:

  6 oz. wild blueberries
  6 oz. vanilla yogurt
  1 Tbs. honey
  ½ c. ice (3 ice cubes)

Directions:

  1. Place all ingredients in blender, and process on high speed until smooth.
  2. Serve immediately.

Yields: 1 serving.

Hot Pink Lemonade

This lemonade is tart and sweet with a boost of antioxidants from the blueberries. The finished drink is hot pink, almost purple.

Ingredients:

    1   c. water
    2   c. sugar
    2¼ c. fresh lemon juice
    7   c. cool water
    2   c. ice
    ¾   c. blueberries

Directions:

1. Boil the 1 cup water with sugar in saucepan over medium-high heat, stirring until liquid becomes clear.
2. Remove from heat and stir in lemon juice.
3. Pour cool water and ice into serving pitcher.
4. Add lemon syrup and blueberries; stir until it turns hot pink.

Yields: 3 quarts.

Blueberry Chocolate Cream Coffee

Serve this drink in front of a fire on a cold winter's eve. It will warm you up deliciously.

Ingredients:

    8 Tbs. blueberry syrup (recipe page 200)
    4 Tbs. chocolate syrup
    1 c. heavy cream, reserve 4 Tbs.
    3 c. hot coffee
    4 sprinkles ground cinnamon
    4 pinches grated orange peel
      Sweetened Whipped Cream (recipe page 238)

Directions:

1. Whip together syrups and cream; reserve 4 tablespoons of cream.
2. Stir reserved cream and blueberry syrup blend in saucepan over low heat until mixed together.
3. Add coffee gradually while stirring mixture.
4. Pour evenly into 4 warmed mugs; top with whipped cream, a sprinkle of cinnamon, and a pinch of grated orange peel.

Yields: 4 servings.

Banana Berry Drink

If you are in a hurry for breakfast, try this cold, refreshing beverage.

Ingredients:

¾ c. orange juice, chilled
⅓ c. pineapple juice, chilled
1 c. frozen blueberries
½ c. frozen sweetened, sliced strawberries
½ c. plain yogurt
1 sm. ripe banana, sliced

Directions:

1. Place half of each ingredient in blender; cover and process until smooth.
2. Pour into chilled glasses.
3. Repeat with remaining ingredients.
4. Serve immediately.

Yields: 5 servings.

Imagination Punch

This tasty punch has ice cube "faces" floating in it. Its blue color makes it a good choice for 4th of July gatherings.

Ingredients for ice cubes:

    18 disposable plastic cups (3-oz. size)
    18 maraschino cherries
    36 fresh blueberries
    1½ c. cold distilled water, divided

Ingredients for punch:

    2   pkg. berry blue gelatin (3 oz. each)
    2   c. boiling water
    4   c. cold water
    2   c. unsweetened pineapple juice
    1   can frozen lemonade concentrate (12 oz.), thawed
    2   liters ginger ale, chilled

Directions for ice cubes:

1. Place plastic cups in muffin pans.
2. From each cherry, cut out a mouth shape; pat dry.
3. Place one cherry mouth and two blueberries for eyes in bottom of each cup.
4. Pour 1 teaspoon distilled water into each cup.
5. Freeze for 30 minutes or until solid.
6. Pour 1 tablespoon distilled water into each cup.
7. Return to freezer; freeze for 3 hours or until solid.

Directions for punch:

1. In large bowl dissolve gelatin in boiling water.
2. Stir in cold water, pineapple juice, and lemonade concentrate.
3. Refrigerate for 1½ hours or until chilled.

4. Just before serving, transfer to 5-quart punch bowl; stir in ginger ale.
5. Remove ice cubes from cups; place face side up in punch bowl.

Yields: 18 servings (about 1 gallon).

Chocoberry Milk Chiller

Chocolate and blueberries blend to form a cool, rich, refreshing drink.

Ingredients:
- 1 c. chocolate milk
- 4 Tbs. chocolate syrup, divided
- 2 Tbs. blueberry syrup (recipe page 200)
  - multicolored sprinkles (optional)
  - fresh or frozen blueberries (optional)

Directions:
1. Stir 2 tablespoons chocolate syrup and 2 tablespoons blueberry syrup into chocolate milk, and mix thoroughly.
2. Chill mixture in freezer for 5 minutes.
3. While mixture is chilling, dip rims of 2 chilled glasses upside down into remaining chocolate syrup then sprinkles to coat edges if desired.
4. Drizzle remaining chocolate syrup on inside and bottom of glasses.
5. Pull mixture out of freezer; pour into chocolate-drizzled glasses.
6. Garnish with blueberries if desired.

Yields: 2 servings.

Blueberry Velvet Cheesecake Smoothie

For a lower fat version, you may use low fat or nonfat yogurt and cream cheese.

Ingredients:

- 1   c. blueberry yogurt (8-oz. container)
- ½   c. grape juice
- ¼   c. cream cheese
- 1   Tbs. maple syrup
- 2½ c. individually frozen blueberries

Directions:

1. Place all ingredients in blender or food processor, and whirl until smooth.

Yields: 2 servings.

Banana Blueberry Smoothie

This smoothie is healthy as well as tasty.

Ingredients:

- 1 c. soy milk
- 1 c. unsweetened blueberries, fresh or frozen
- 1 lg. banana
- 1 tsp. flaxseed

Directions:

1. In blender container combine soy milk, blueberries, banana, and flaxseed.
2. Blend until smooth.

Yields: 1 serving.

Saturn Slush

The swirled blueberry and strawberry layers in this beverage may remind you of Saturn's rings. The garnish has a space theme, too.

Ingredients:

    1 pkg. frozen unsweetened strawberries (20 oz.), unthawed

    3 c. orange juice, divided

    ¾ c. confectioners' sugar, divided

    2 c. frozen blueberries

    6 fresh strawberries, hulled, halved widthwise

    6 unpeeled orange slices

Directions:

1. In blender combine frozen strawberries, 2 cups of orange juice, and ½ cup of confectioners' sugar.
2. Cover and process until smooth; set aside.
3. Rinse blender container.
4. Add blueberries and remaining juice and sugar; cover and blend until smooth.
5. Alternate layers of strawberry and blueberry in glasses; stir layers a few times to create a swirl.
6. For garnish, thread a strawberry top (hulled side first), an orange slice, and a strawberry tip (cut side first) onto a drinking straw or stirring stick; place in glass.

Yields: 6 servings.

Did You Know? . . . .

Did you know that the Maine blueberry crop requires about 50,000 beehives for pollination, with most of the hives being trucked in from other states for that purpose?

Kiwi Blueberry Smoothie

There are many smoothie variations. The kiwifruit in this version is a special treat.

Ingredients:

- 3   kiwifruit, peeled, cut into chunks
- 2   med. ripe bananas, cut into 4 pieces and frozen
- 1   c. frozen blueberries
- 8   oz. plain yogurt
- 3   Tbs. honey
- ¼   tsp. almond extract (optional)
- 1½ c. crushed ice

Directions:

1. In blender combine fruit, yogurt, honey, and extract if desired; cover and process until combined.
2. Add ice; cover and process until blended, stirring if necessary.
3. Pour into chilled glasses; serve immediately.

Yields: 4 servings.

Bloody Bug Juice

You can have lots of fun with this recipe. Children, especially, will love it.

Ingredients:

- 24 oz. frozen strawberries, thawed
- 6   oz. lemonade frozen concentrate
- 1   qt. ginger ale
- 1   c. raisins
- 1   c. blueberries, fresh or frozen

Directions:

1. Place strawberries in bowl and mash with fork.
2. In large pitcher mix strawberry mash, lemonade, and ginger ale.
3. Place handfuls of raisins and blueberries (bugs) into tall glasses.
4. Pour liquid over bugs, then sit back and watch the bugs and scum rise to the top of each glass.
5. Double or triple this recipe and serve in a punch bowl for a party, draping gummy worms over rim of bowl for added effect.

Yields: 6 servings.

Blueberry Café au Lait

Try this recipe for a new variation on a favorite coffee drink.

Ingredients:

⅔ c. hot coffee
2 Tbs. blueberry syrup (recipe page 200)
⅓ c. milk
  cinnamon, nutmeg, or chocolate powder (optional)

Directions:

1. Pour hot coffee into warmed mug.
2. Stir in blueberry syrup.
3. Steam and froth milk; add to coffee, leaving layer of foam on top.
4. Sprinkle cinnamon, nutmeg, or chocolate powder on top of foam if desired.
5. Serve immediately.

Yields: 1 serving.

Blueberry Tofu Smoothie

This smoothie is great for vegetarians because of its use of tofu instead of yogurt or milk.

Ingredients:

    ¼ pack tofu
    ½ c. blueberries
    ½ c. ice
    2 Tbs. sugar (optional)
      water or juice as needed

Directions:

1. Place all ingredients in blender, and process until smooth.

Yields: 1 serving.

Berry Slush

A slush can be so refreshing on a hot summer day.

Ingredients:

1   pkg. berry blue or raspberry gelatin (3 oz.)
2   c. boiling water
2   c. sugar
1   can pineapple juice (46 oz.)
2   liters ginger ale
4½ c. cold water
1   c. lemon juice
    blue or red liquid food coloring (optional)
    fresh raspberries, blueberries, and star fruit

Directions:

1. In large container dissolve gelatin in boiling water; stir in sugar until dissolved.
2. Add pineapple juice, ginger ale, water, and lemon juice; add food coloring if desired.
3. Freeze for 8 hours or overnight.
4. Remove from freezer 20 minutes before serving; stir so mixture will be slushy.
5. Serve in chilled glasses.
6. For garnish thread fruit on wooden skewers.
7. Serve immediately

Yields: 5 quarts.

Fruit Slush

This is another refreshing slush. It is also lower in sugar than other recipes. You can experiment with different fruits to make your favorite flavor combination.

Ingredients:

5 frozen unsweetened whole strawberries
1 c. frozen blueberries
1 can frozen orange juice concentrate (6 oz.)
½ c. canned peaches in extra-light syrup
½ c. sugar
¾ c. water
2 Tbs. lemon juice

Directions:

1. Place all ingredients in food processor or blender; cover and process until smooth.
2. Pour into chilled glasses; serve immediately.

Yields: 4 servings.

Blueberry Iced Spiced Tea

This makes a refreshing iced tea on a hot day with the addition of cinnamon and ginger. Serve it with cinnamon sticks for swizzles.

Ingredients:

   6 c. water
  12 blueberry herbal tea bags
   2 cinnamon sticks (3-in. lengths)
   1 Tbs. fresh ginger, minced
   1 c. cranberry juice
     sugar to taste
     crushed ice
     cinnamon sticks for swizzles

Directions:

1. Heat water in large saucepan just to boiling point.
2. Add tea bags, cinnamon sticks, and ginger.
3. Remove from heat, cover, and let steep about 15 minutes.
4. Add juice and sugar to taste.
5. Strain tea into pitcher; cover and chill.
6. Pour tea into glasses of crushed ice, and serve garnished with cinnamon sticks as swizzles.

Yields: 6 to 8 servings.

Did You Know? . . . .

Did you know that the Northern Highbush Blueberry was introduced into British Columbia and the state of Washington and, even farther afield, into Great Britain and Australia?

Blueberry Delights Cookbook

A Collection of Blueberry Recipes
Cookbook Delights Series-Book 2

Breads and Rolls

Table of Contents

Page

Did You Know? . . . .

Did you know that premium blueberry jam, usually made from wild blueberries, is common in Maine, Ontario, Quebec, and British Columbia?

Dried Blueberry and Spice Swirl Bread

As a change of pace from cinnamon-raisin bread, try this blueberry bread.

Ingredients:

    4-5 c. all-purpose flour
    1   c. rolled oats
    ¼   c. non-fat dry milk
    2   pkg. active dry yeast
    2   tsp. salt
    1½   c. water
    ½   c. light molasses
    2   Tbs. oil
    1   egg
    2   Tbs. butter, melted
    3   Tbs. sugar
    1½   Tbs. ground cinnamon
    1½   c. dried blueberries (recipe page 253)

Directions:

1. In large bowl stir together 1 cup flour, oats, dry milk, yeast, and salt; set aside.
2. Heat water, molasses, and oil until very warm, 120 to 130 degrees F.
3. Pour warm liquid over flour-yeast mixture in large bowl.
4. Add egg and beat with electric mixer on low speed for 3 minutes.
5. By hand, stir in 3 cups of flour.
6. When dough can be handled, remove from bowl and knead with hands for 5 to 7 minutes, incorporating remaining cup of flour if needed, until dough is firm yet smooth.
7. Place in greased bowl, cover with greased wax paper, and let rest in warm, humid place free from drafts until doubled in size, about 1 hour.
8. Thoroughly grease two 8½ x 4½-inch loaf pans; set aside.
9. Punch down dough and divide in half.
10. Roll each half into 8 x 16-inch rectangle.

11. Brush each half with melted butter.
12. Combine sugar and cinnamon and sprinkle over halves, then sprinkle dried blueberries evenly over cinnamon mixture.
13. Starting at short end, roll each half tightly.
14. With seam sides down, place in prepared pans.
15. Cover and let rest in warm, humid place until doubled in size, about 1 hour.
16. Preheat oven to 375 degrees F.
17. Bake for 40 to 45 minutes or until bread is golden brown and sounds hollow when tapped.
18. Remove bread from pans, and allow to cool on wire racks.

Yields: 2 loaves.

Frosty Blueberry Fritters

These fritters are especially tasty when hot.

Ingredients:

1½ c. all-purpose flour
¾ c. sugar
3   tsp. baking powder
¾ c. fresh blueberries
1   egg, beaten
1   c. milk
    oil for frying
    confectioners' sugar

Directions:

1. Heat oil for deep frying to 375 degrees F.
2. Sift together dry ingredients; add berries.
3. Mix egg and milk and add to dry mixture, mixing just until moistened.
4. Drop batter by tablespoonfuls into hot oil.
5. Fry until golden brown, 3 to 4 minutes, turning once.
6. Drain on paper towel.
7. Sprinkle with confectioners' sugar.

Health Nut Blueberry Muffins

The title says it all. These muffins are made with a wealth of healthy ingredients.

Ingredients:

   ¾ c. all-purpose flour or whole-wheat pastry flour
   ¾ c. whole-wheat flour
   ¾ c. brown sugar, firmly packed
   ¼ c. oat bran
   ¼ c. quick-cooking oats
   ¼ c. wheat germ
   1 tsp. baking powder
   1 tsp. baking soda
   ¼ tsp. salt
   1 c. blueberries
   ½ c. chopped walnuts
   1 banana, mashed
   1 c. buttermilk
   1 egg
   1 Tbs. vegetable oil
   1 tsp. vanilla extract

Directions:

1. Preheat oven to 350 degrees F.
2. Oil 12-cup muffin pan or line with paper muffin cups.
3. In large bowl stir together flours, sugar, oat bran, quick-cooking oats, wheat germ, baking powder, baking soda, and salt.
4. Gently stir in blueberries and walnuts.
5. In separate bowl mix together mashed banana, buttermilk, egg, oil, and vanilla.
6. Pour wet ingredients into dry, and mix just until blended.
7. Spoon into muffin cups, filling all the way to top.
8. Bake for 15 to 18 minutes or until tops of muffins spring back when lightly touched.

Yields: 12 muffins.

Blueberry Nut Bread

This is a nice nut bread, and with the addition of blueberries, it will have a nice purple color.

Ingredients:

- 3   c. all-purpose flour
- 1   Tbs. baking powder
- ¼   tsp. baking soda
- ½   tsp. ground nutmeg
- ¾   c. sugar
- 3   lg. eggs
- 2   tsp. vanilla extract
- ½   c. milk
- ½   c. butter, melted
- 1½ tsp. orange extract
- ⅓   c. orange juice
- 3   c. blueberries, fresh or frozen
- 1⅓ c. chopped nuts (walnuts or pecans)

Directions:

1. Preheat oven to 350 degrees F.
2. Combine flour, baking soda, nutmeg, and sugar.
3. Beat eggs, milk, vanilla, melted butter, orange extract, and orange juice.
4. Pour into dry ingredients and mix well.
5. Add blueberries and nuts.
6. Stir thoroughly but gently.
7. Pour into well-buttered mini loaf pans, and set aside for 15 minutes.
8. Bake 45 minutes for small loaves, or 75 minutes for a large loaf, or until done.

Yields: 4 mini loaves or 2 large loaves.

Cornbread Sticks with Blueberries

The added touch of blueberries makes these cornbread sticks very tasty.

Ingredients:

- 1   c. milk
- 1   egg
- 1   c. yellow cornmeal
- 1   c. all-purpose flour
- 2   Tbs. sugar
- 1   Tbs. baking powder
- ½   tsp. salt
- 1¼ c. blueberries

Directions:

1. Preheat oven and cast iron pans to 425 degree F.
2. Beat milk and egg until blended.
3. Sift together cornmeal, flour, sugar, baking powder, and salt.
4. Add blueberries to dry ingredients.
5. Combine liquid and dry ingredients, stirring just until moistened.
6. Remove pans from oven, and brush or spray with oil or baking spray.
7. Pour batter into iron pans.
8. Return to oven and bake 15 to 20 minutes.
9. Remove from oven and cut into long sticks to serve.

Did You Know? . . . .

Did you know that if all the blueberries grown in North America in one year were spread out in a single layer, they would cover a four-lane highway stretching from New York to Chicago?

Blueberry Banana Nut Bread

This is a moist and delicious alternative variety of the traditional banana nut bread.

Ingredients:

- 1¾ c. sifted all-purpose flour
- 2 tsp. baking powder
- ¼ tsp. baking soda
- 1 pinch of salt
- ⅓ c. butter, softened
- ⅔ c. sugar
- 2 eggs
- 1 c. bananas, mashed
- ½ c. chopped walnuts or pecans
- 1½ c. blueberries

Directions:

1. Preheat oven to 350 degrees F.
2. Sift together flour, baking powder, soda, and salt.
3. In another bowl cream butter; gradually beat in sugar until light and fluffy.
4. Add eggs one at a time, mixing well after each addition.
5. Add flour mixture and banana alternately in 3 parts.
6. Stir in walnuts, and then gently stir in blueberries.
7. Pour into oiled 9 x 5-inch loaf pan.
8. Bake for 50 minutes.
9. Remove from pan and cool on wire rack.

Did You Know? . . . .

Did you know that the North American blueberry industry ships more than 100 metric tons of fresh blueberries each year to Iceland and more than 500 metric tons to Japan?

Blueberry Buttermilk Biscuits

Nothing beats the delicious taste of fresh, warm buttermilk biscuits, and the added flavor of blueberries makes them even more desirable.

Ingredients:

- 2 c. all-purpose flour
- 1 Tbs. baking powder
- ¼ tsp. baking soda
- 1 tsp. salt
- ½ c. plus 3 Tbs. sugar, divided
- 1 tsp. grated orange rind
- ⅓ c. butter
- 1 egg, beaten
- ¾ c. buttermilk
- ½ c. blueberries, fresh or frozen
- 3 Tbs. melted butter
- ⅛ tsp. ground cinnamon
- 1 dash ground nutmeg

Directions:

1. Preheat oven to 400 degrees F.
2. In medium bowl mix flour, baking powder, baking soda, salt, ½ cup sugar, and orange rind together.
3. Using pastry cutter or two knives, cut butter into flour mixture until it resembles coarse meal.
4. In small bowl lightly beat egg with fork.
5. Add buttermilk to beaten egg, and then add it to flour mixture.
6. Using fork, stir until just moistened.
7. Add blueberries, stirring gently just to mix.
8. Turn dough out onto floured surface or cloth, and gently knead 3 or 4 times.
9. Roll out to ½-inch thickness; cut with biscuit cutter or into desired shapes.

10. Place on lightly greased cookie sheet, and bake for 15 minutes or until golden.
11. Mix butter with remaining 3 tablespoons sugar, cinnamon, and nutmeg, and brush onto tops of biscuits as they come from the oven.

Yields: 12 to 15 biscuits.

Blueberry Bread

This is tasty bread for a quick snack.

Ingredients:

1¾ c. sugar
3 c. sifted all-purpose flour
1½ tsp. baking soda
1 Tbs. ground cinnamon
¾ tsp. salt
1¼ c. oil
4 eggs, beaten
2 c. frozen blueberries, drained

Directions:

1. Preheat oven to 350 degrees F.
2. Mix sugar, flour, soda, cinnamon, and salt.
3. Add oil and eggs; stir until mixed well.
4. Gently stir in blueberries.
5. Pour into 2 bread pans sprayed with nonstick cooking spray, and bake for 1 hour.
6. Remove from oven and invert onto wire rack, then turn right side up to cool.
7. Slice and serve.

Yields: 2 loaves.

Blueberry Cornbread

Try this blueberry cornbread warm out of the oven with your next meal.

Ingredients:

- ½ c. butter, softened
- 1 c. sugar
- 2 eggs
- 1 c. yellow cornmeal
- 1½ c. all-purpose flour
- 2 Tbs. baking powder
- ½ tsp. salt
- 1½ c. milk
- ½ c. blueberries

Directions:

1. Preheat oven to 375 degrees F.
2. With electric mixer, cream butter with sugar.
3. Add eggs and cornmeal; mix well.
4. Sift flour, baking powder, and salt onto sheet of wax paper.
5. Add flour and milk alternately to creamed mixture, mixing just until moistened.
6. Coat blueberries with flour and stir into mixture.
7. Pour into 8-inch square pan, greased or lined with wax paper.
8. Bake for 40 minutes or until wooden pick inserted near center comes out clean.
9. Remove from oven and cut into squares.
10. Serve warm with butter.

Did You Know? . . . .

Did you know that the blueberry is the second most popular berry in the U.S.? The strawberry is number one.

Blueberry Mandarin Orange Muffins

These are a tasty version of muffins. The pecans give them a nice nutty flavor.

Ingredients:

3   c. Mandarin orange segments, halved
1   Tbs. orange or vanilla extract
6   c. cake flour
2⅓ Tbs. baking powder
1   Tbs. baking soda
¼   tsp. salt
1½ c. brown sugar, firmly packed
¾   c. sugar
3   eggs
3   c. plain yogurt
½   c. canola oil
1   c. chopped pecans
1½ lb. blueberries

Directions:

1. Preheat oven to 400 degrees F., and grease muffin tins.
2. In small bowl combine orange segments and vanilla; set aside.
3. In large bowl combine flour, baking powder, baking soda, and salt; set aside.
4. In another bowl combine sugars, eggs, yogurt, and oil.
5. Stir into dry mixture and mix just until moistened.
6. Fold in orange mixture, blueberries, and pecans.
7. Scoop ¼ cup batter into each greased muffin cup.
8. Bake 18 to 22 minutes or until firm to the touch.
9. Remove from oven, turn out onto wire rack, and serve warm.

Yields: 36 muffins.

Blueberry Cinnamon Rolls

Sweet wild blueberries wrapped inside tender dough topped with a glaze make an excellent, tasty treat. You can make these terrific rolls with huckleberries, too.

Ingredients for rolls:

¼ c. milk
¼ c. sugar
½ tsp. salt
3 Tbs. butter
1 pkg. dry yeast
¼ c. warm water (105 to 115 degrees F.)
2¼ c. all-purpose flour, divided
1 egg
2 Tbs. butter, softened
¼ c. brown sugar, firmly packed
½ c. blueberries, fresh or frozen
1 Tbs. butter, melted

Ingredients for glaze:

1 c. confectioners' sugar, sifted
2 Tbs. milk

Directions for rolls:

1. Combine milk, sugar, salt, and 3 tablespoons butter in saucepan; heat until butter melts.
2. Cool to 105 to 115 degrees F.
3. Dissolve yeast in warm water in large mixing bowl; let stand 5 minutes.
4. Stir in milk mixture, 1½ cups flour, and egg; beat at medium speed of electric mixer until smooth.
5. Stir in remaining ¾ cup flour.
6. Turn dough onto lightly floured surface, and knead until smooth and elastic, about 8 minutes.

7. Place in well-greased bowl, turning to grease top.
8. Cover and let rise in warm place (85 degrees F.), free from drafts, for 1 hour (dough will not quite double in bulk).
9. Punch dough down, and turn out onto lightly floured surface.
10. Roll dough into 12 x 8-inch rectangle; spread with 2 tablespoons softened butter.
11. Combine brown sugar and cinnamon; sprinkle mixture over rectangle, then sprinkle with blueberries.
12. Roll dough jellyroll fashion, starting at long side.
13. Pinch seam to seal; do not seal ends.
14. Cut roll into 1-inch slices; place slices cut side down in buttered 8-inch square pan.
15. Brush tops with 1 tablespoon melted butter.
16. Using fork, gently lift center of rolls to form peak.
17. Cover and let rise in warm place, free from drafts, about 40 minutes (rolls will not double in bulk).
18. Preheat oven to 350 degrees F.
19. Bake for 35 minutes.

Directions for glaze:
1. Combine confectioners' sugar and 2 tablespoons milk, stirring well.
2. Drizzle over warm rolls.

Yields: About 8 rolls.

Did You Know? . . . .

Did you know that at least 50 different species of blueberries have been identified?

Blueberry Flatbread

This blueberry flatbread is a cross between a cookie and a pancake. The batter is spread out very thin on a baking sheet, quickly baked, broken apart into pieces, and then eaten hot.

Ingredients:

- 2 c. all-purpose flour
- 1 Tbs. baking powder
- 3 Tbs. sugar
- ¾ tsp. salt
- 8 Tbs. cold, unsalted butter
- 1 lg. egg
- ¾ c. plus 1 Tbs. milk
- 1 c. blueberries, rinsed, stemmed
- 1 Tbs. ground cinnamon mixed with ¼ c. sugar

Directions:

1. Heat oven to 450 degrees F.; place rack in center of oven.
2. Spray large baking sheet with nonstick cooking spray.
3. In medium bowl stir together flour, baking powder, sugar, and salt.
4. Cut in butter with 2 table knives or wire pastry blender until it is size of peas; set aside.
5. Beat egg in small bowl, and then beat in milk.
6. Add berries to dry ingredients, then add egg mixture all at once; stir just until moistened.
7. Do not over mix; dough will be sticky.
8. Pat out ½ inches thick on baking sheet, about 9 x 12 inches.
9. Sprinkle on cinnamon-sugar.
10. Bake for about 12 minutes.
11. Break apart and serve hot.

Wild Blueberry Scones

These scones are great served warm from the oven with butter and honey, or for a traditional flavor, serve them with cream and jam.

Ingredients:

    2 c. all-purpose flour
    3 tsp. baking powder
    1 pinch salt
    3 Tbs. sugar
    ½ tsp. ground allspice
    5 Tbs. butter, softened
    ½ c. milk
    ½ c. blueberries
       sugar for glaze (optional)

Directions:

1. Preheat oven to 425 degrees F.
2. Grease large baking sheet.
3. Combine flour, baking powder, salt, sugar, and allspice in large bowl.
4. Cut in butter with pastry knife or fork until crumbly.
5. Make well in center and add milk; stir several strokes, add wild blueberries, then stir just until dough forms.
6. Add a sprinkle more of milk if dough does not stick together, but be careful not to overwork dough.
7. Form into ball and flatten into 9- or 10-inch disk.
8. Using sharp, long-bladed knife, cut dough into 8 or 10 pie-shaped wedges.
9. You can either slide dough onto baking sheet as is for scones shaped in wedges, or separate the pieces and push them into slightly flattened balls for scones shaped in circles.
10. For either shape, brush tops with milk and sprinkles some sugar on each.
11. Bake 12 to 15 minutes or until golden brown.
12. Remove from oven and serve hot.

Black and Blueberry Muffins

These moist, sweet muffins are full of berries. They are a healthy treat since they are also made with whole-wheat flour and wheat germ.

Ingredients:

    1 c. whole-wheat flour
    1 c. all-purpose flour
    ⅓ c. wheat germ
    ⅔ c. brown sugar, firmly packed
    1 Tbs. baking powder
    1 tsp. salt
    1 tsp. ground cinnamon
    2 eggs, beaten
    2 c. half-and-half
    1 c. fresh blackberries
    1 c. fresh blueberries

Directions:

1. Preheat oven to 400 degrees F.
2. Butter muffin pans or line with paper cups.
3. In large mixing bowl whisk together flours, wheat germ, sugar, baking powder, salt, and cinnamon.
4. In another bowl whisk together half-and-half and eggs.
5. Stir wet ingredients into dry, mixing just to combine; fold in berries.
6. Scoop batter into muffin pan cups. (If there are any empty cups, fill them halfway with water.)
7. Bake for 20 minutes or until done.

Yields: 18 muffins.

Blueberry Delights Cookbook
A Collection of Blueberry Recipes
Cookbook Delights Series-Book 2

Breakfasts

Table of Contents

Page

Did You Know? . . . .

Did you know that the blueberry is the official berry of Nova Scotia?

French-Style Croissants with Blueberry Sauce

Try something different and use croissants instead of French toast.

Ingredients for sauce:

12 oz. frozen blueberries
¼ c. sugar
½ c. water
½ c. blueberry jam (recipe page 194)

Ingredients for fried croissants:

4 croissants, cut in half
2 eggs, beaten, in flat dish
3 Tbs. butter
Sweetened Whipped Cream (recipe page 238)

Directions for sauce:

1. Combine blueberries, sugar, water, and blueberry jam in saucepan.
2. Simmer over medium heat for approximately 20 to 30 minutes or just until thickened, stirring occasionally.
3. Remove from heat, and keep warm while preparing croissants.
4. This sauce may be stored in refrigerator and also used to top ice cream, pound cake, pancakes, waffles, or French toast.

Directions for fried croissants:

1. Heat butter to bubbling in frying pan or griddle.
2. Whisk eggs and milk together with fork.
3. Dip both sides of bottom half of croissant and only inside of top half in egg mixture.
4. Brown sides that have egg mixture on them in frying pan until golden.
5. Turn bottom only once, cooking until browned; do not turn top half, leaving it to stay dry and attractive.

6. Place bottom half of cooked croissant on plate.
7. Top with 2 tablespoons warm blueberry sauce.
8. Place top half of croissant slightly askew over bottom half.
9. Use 2 more tablespoons of blueberry sauce to drizzle over top half.
10. Top with whipped cream and serve immediately.

Yields: 4 servings.

Cranberry Orange-Spiced Oatmeal

This wonderful microwave recipe is made with plenty of oats and cinnamon for a warm, tasty breakfast.

Ingredients:
¾ c. old-fashioned rolled oats
½ tsp. ground cinnamon or to taste
¼ c. dried cranberries
½ c. frozen blueberries
¼ tsp. ground turmeric (optional)
1 pinch ground ginger (optional)
1 c. water
¼ c. orange juice or as needed

Directions:
1. Place rolled oats, cinnamon, cranberries, and blueberries in microwave-safe bowl.
2. Add turmeric and ginger if desired.
3. Pour in water and stir to mix ingredients.
4. Cook on high until water is absorbed, about 2 minutes.
5. Stir in orange juice to desired consistency.

Yields: 1 serving.

Blueberry Granola Bars

Granola bars are handy to have on hand when you have to eat breakfast on the run. They are a healthy after-school snack, too.

Ingredients:

- ½ c. honey
- ¼ c. brown sugar, firmly packed
- 3 Tbs. vegetable oil
- 1½ tsp. ground cinnamon
- 1½ c. quick-cooking oats
- 2 c. fresh blueberries

Directions:

1. Preheat oven to 350 degrees F.
2. Lightly grease 9-inch square baking pan.
3. In medium saucepan combine honey, brown sugar, oil, and cinnamon; bring to a boil.
4. Continue boiling for 2 minutes; do not stir.
5. In large mixing bowl combine oats and blueberries.
6. Stir in honey mixture until thoroughly blended.
7. Spread onto prepared baking pan, gently pressing mixture flat.
8. Bake until lightly browned, about 40 minutes.
9. Cool completely in pan on wire rack.
10. Cut into 1½ x 3-inch bars.

Yields: 18 bars.

Did You Know? . . . .

Did you know that a ½-cup serving of blueberries delivers as much antioxidant power as five servings of peas, carrots, squash, or broccoli, as well as other foods tested?

Blueberry Breakfast Custard

This is an interesting combination of cheese and blueberries in an egg custard. Serve with toast or your favorite muffins.

Ingredients:

- 5 eggs
- 3 Tbs. melted butter
- 1 tsp. cornstarch
- ⅛ tsp. baking powder
- ¼ tsp. salt
- ¼ tsp. pepper
- ¼ tsp. dried mustard
- 1¼ c. milk
- ⅔ c. shredded cheddar cheese
- blueberries

Directions:

1. Preheat oven to 425 degrees F.
2. In medium bowl beat eggs well.
3. Add butter, cornstarch, baking powder, salt, pepper, and dried mustard to eggs.
4. Blend in milk.
5. Divide cheese among 4 individual custard dishes.
6. Pour mixture evenly into custard dishes.
7. Place custard dishes into baking pan, and fill pan with boiling water 1 inch deep.
8. Bake, uncovered, for 15 to 20 minutes.
9. Top with fresh blueberries and serve immediately.

Yields: 4 servings.

Blueberry Buttermilk Pancakes

These buttermilk pancakes are full of blueberries and are easy to make. Make plenty because they will disappear quickly.

Ingredients:

- ¾ c. plus 1 Tbs. all-purpose flour
- ½ tsp. baking soda
- ½ tsp. salt
- 2 lg. eggs
- 2 Tbs. sugar
- 1 c. buttermilk
- 1 tsp. vanilla extract
- 4 Tbs. unsalted butter, melted, cooled, divided
- 3¾ c. fresh blueberries, divided
- confectioners' sugar
- warm blueberry syrup (recipe page 200)

Directions:

1. Sift together flour, baking soda, and salt into medium mixing bowl.
2. In small bowl lightly beat eggs with sugar, then stir in buttermilk, vanilla, and 2 tablespoons melted butter.
3. Add wet ingredients to flour mixture, and stir until just moistened. (Batter should have consistency of thick cream with some lumps. Do not over mix.)
4. Heat large griddle or 2 large nonstick skillets over medium-high heat, brushing each lightly with some of remaining melted butter.
5. Gently pour ¼ cup batter onto skillet or griddle, 2 inches apart.
6. Using 1¾ cups of the blueberries, press a few blueberries into each pancake, and cook until undersides are golden brown and bubbles are breaking on top, about 1½ minutes; turn and cook another 1½ minutes.

7. Keep pancakes warm in oven on low as you cook remaining batter.
8. Divide pancakes among warmed plates and top with remaining 2 cups blueberries.
9. Sprinkle with confectioners' sugar, and serve with warm blueberry or maple syrup.

Blueberry Waffles

Blueberries are a delicious addition to waffles. Serve these hot with homemade blueberry syrup.

Ingredients:

1½ c. all-purpose flour
3   tsp. baking powder
½   tsp. salt
3   eggs, separated
1½ c. buttermilk
6   Tbs. butter, melted
2   Tbs. brown sugar
1   c. blueberries

Directions:

1. Sift together flour, baking powder, and salt.
2. Beat egg yolks, and combine with buttermilk and melted butter; beat in flour mixture.
3. Beat egg whites until stiff; add sugar and beat again.
4. Fold into batter and gently stir in blueberries.
5. Grease waffle irons well and preheat to very hot.
6. Prepare waffles, and serve with blueberry sauce and/or whipped cream.

Blueberry Cornmeal Cake

This makes a flavorful breakfast cake. Blueberries and cornbread actually make a great-tasting combination.

Ingredients:

   1 c. plus 2 Tbs. self-rising flour
   ¾ c. fine cornmeal
   ⅛ tsp. salt
   ¾ c. unsalted butter, softened
   ⅔ c. plus 3 Tbs. sugar, divided
   1 egg
   2 c. blueberries, lightly rinsed, dried
   1 Tbs. confectioners' sugar for dusting

Directions:

   1. Preheat oven to 375 degrees F.
   2. Sift flour, cornmeal, and salt together in medium bowl; set aside.
   3. Beat butter and ⅔ cup sugar using electric mixer at medium speed.
   4. Add egg and beat well.
   5. Add flour mixture at low speed, and mix until just blended.
   6. Press ¾ of dough evenly over bottom of 8½-inch springform pan and about 1 inch up side.
   7. Toss blueberries in bowl with remaining 3 tablespoons sugar; pour berries over dough in pan.
   8. Top blueberries with remaining dough, pinching off small amounts and arranging it evenly over surface.
   9. Bake cake in center of oven until nicely browned, 40 to 50 minutes, covering top with aluminum foil if it browns too quickly.

10. Cool in pan on rack for 1 to 2 hours before slicing so it holds together well.
11. Just before serving, dust with confectioners' sugar and remove sides of pan.

Fruited Sausage

This glazed combination of sausage and fruit is a welcome addition to any breakfast buffet. You can stretch it by adding whatever fruit you have on hand, such as apples, peaches, or cranberries. It can also be served over noodles or rice as a skillet supper.

Ingredients:

1 pkg. fully cooked kielbasa or Polish sausage (16 oz.)
1 can pineapple chunks (20 oz.), undrained
¼ cup brown sugar, firmly packed
2 Tbs. cornstarch
1 can Mandarin oranges (11 oz.), drained
1 c. blueberries, fresh or frozen

Directions:

1. Cut sausage into chunks.
2. In large skillet bring pineapple and sausage to a boil.
3. Combine brown sugar and cornstarch; add to skillet.
4. Stir in oranges and blueberries.
5. Return to a boil; cook and stir for 1 to 2 minutes or until thickened.

Yields: 5 servings.

Blueberry French Toast

My daughter loves French toast, and this makes an enjoyable variation of the classic version.

Ingredients:

    2 c. frozen blueberries
    ¾ c. maple syrup
    1 tsp. grated orange zest
    1 Tbs. cornstarch
    2 Tbs. water
    4 eggs, beaten
    ¾ c. milk
    1 tsp. vanilla extract
    ¼ tsp. ground nutmeg
    8 slices bread
    4 Tbs. butter
    confectioners' sugar

Directions:

1. Combine blueberries, maple syrup, and orange zest in small saucepan.
2. Dissolve cornstarch in water and add to blueberry mixture.
3. Cook and stir until mixture boils; reduce heat and simmer 1 minute or until mixture thickens.
4. Combine eggs, milk, vanilla, and nutmeg; mix well.
5. Dip each slice of bread into egg mixture.
6. Cook each slice in small amount of butter in skillet or on griddle about 2 minutes or until golden.
7. Place 1 slice on each individual plate, and spread with 3 tablespoons blueberry mixture.
8. Sprinkle lightly with confectioners' sugar.

Big Blueberry Popover

This popover is a great breakfast treat. Although it is wonderful with blueberries, any berry can be used.

Ingredients:

- 1 c. milk
- ½ tsp. vanilla extract
- 2 Tbs. butter, melted
- ¼ tsp. salt
- ⅛ tsp. fresh ground nutmeg
- ¼ c. sugar, divided
- 1 c. sifted all-purpose flour
- 2 eggs, beaten
- ¼ tsp. ground cinnamon
- 1 c. blueberries or other berries

Directions:

1. Preheat oven to 450 degrees F.; adjust oven rack to middle position.
2. Mix milk, vanilla, butter, salt, nutmeg, and 3 tablespoons sugar in large bowl.
3. Stir in flour then eggs until just combined; let this batter stand for 5 minutes.
4. Meanwhile, mix remaining 1 tablespoon sugar and cinnamon in separate bowl; set aside.
5. Place berries in buttered 9-inch pie pan.
6. Pour batter over berries, and sprinkle cinnamon-sugar over batter.
7. Bake for 20 minutes.
8. Reduce oven temperature to 350 degrees F., and bake until popover is firm and golden brown, 15 to 20 minutes longer.
9. Cut popover into wedges and serve immediately.

Yields: 6 servings.

Blueberry Pancakes

The beaten egg whites in this recipe lighten the texture of the pancakes. These pancakes will disappear quickly. Serve warm with butter and your favorite syrup.

Ingredients:

- 2 lg. eggs, separated into 2 large bowls
- 3 lg. egg whites
- 2 c. plain yogurt
- ½ c. unsweetened applesauce
- ¼ c. sugar
- 1 tsp. vanilla extract
- 2 tsp. baking soda
- ½ tsp. salt
- 1¾ c. all-purpose flour
- ½ tsp. vegetable oil (or more if needed)
- 2 c. blueberries

Directions:

1. Add yogurt, applesauce, sugar, and vanilla to bowl with 2 egg yolks, stirring with rubber spatula to mix.
2. Sift together baking soda, salt, and flour, and add to wet ingredients, mixing just until blended.
3. Beat 5 egg whites with electric mixer until stiff peaks form when beaters are lifted.
4. Stir ⅓ of whites into batter until blended; gently fold in remaining whites until no white streaks remain.
5. Heat griddle or large skillet over medium heat until a few drops of water flicked onto surface skitter and disappear.
6. Brush ½ teaspoon oil over cooking surface.
7. For each pancake, pour ¼ cup batter onto griddle or skillet, gently spreading batter.
8. Quickly sprinkle berries on top, then cook 2 minutes longer or until bubbles appear on surface of pancake and undersides are golden brown.

9. Turn pancakes over with broad metal spatula, and cook until tops bounce back when touched, about 2 minutes.
10. Remove to serving plates, and top with your favorite syrup.

Blueberry Oven Custard Puff Pancake

Our family loves puff pancakes, and the addition of blueberry flavor makes these a great breakfast treat.

Ingredients:

2 Tbs. butter
3 eggs
2 c. milk, divided
¾ c. all-purpose flour
1 Tbs. sugar
½ tsp. salt
2 c. blueberries
¼ tsp. ground cinnamon
confectioners' sugar

Directions:

1. Preheat oven to 425 degrees F.
2. Heat butter in oven in heavy skillet until bubbly.
3. In bowl beat eggs, ¼ cup milk, flour, sugar, and salt until smooth.
4. Beat in remaining milk.
5. Pour into oven-heated skillet.
6. Return to oven and bake for 20 minutes.
7. Sprinkle with berries and cinnamon.
8. Bake 10 to 15 minutes longer, until knife inserted comes out clean and pancake is browned and puffed.
9. Remove from oven, cut into squares, and serve hot on individual serving plates after dusting with confectioners' sugar.

Sour Cream Blueberry Waffles

Try these great-tasting waffles for a nice change.

Ingredients for waffles:

6	eggs
3	c. sour cream
1	c. melted butter
3	c. all-purpose flour
½	c. sugar
1½	tsp. baking soda

Ingredients for sauce:

1	bag frozen strawberries
2	c. orange juice, divided
3	Tbs. cornstarch
1	carton frozen blueberries
½	c. frozen cranberries
	sugar to taste

Directions for waffles:

1. In bowl beat eggs with whisk until light.
2. Fold in sour cream and melted butter.
3. Sift in dry ingredients; blend to lumpy consistency.
4. Spray preheated waffle iron with nonstick cooking spray once before cooking.
5. Use 1 cup mix for 4-section waffle iron.
6. Waffles may be baked and kept warm or baked individually and served immediately with sauce.

Directions for sauce:

1. Heat and stir strawberries, 1½ cups orange juice, and sugar in saucepan over low heat until warm.
2. Combine remaining ½ cup orange juice and cornstarch; add to saucepan, and cook until mixture has thickened.

3. Remove from heat; add blueberries and cranberries, folding in gently to keep berries whole.
4. Spoon over hot waffles and serve.

Banana Blueberry Nut Bran Muffins

Nuts and bran cereal make this a healthy and flavorful muffin.

Ingredients:

1½ c. sugar
4   ripe bananas, puréed
3   c. frozen blueberries
1   c. chopped walnuts
1½ tsp. vanilla extract
2   eggs
3   tsp. baking soda
2   c. oat bran
4   c. bran cereal
2½ c. unsifted all-purpose flour
1   qt. buttermilk

Directions:

1. Preheat oven to 375 degrees F.
2. In large bowl combine sugar, bananas, blueberries, nuts, vanilla, and eggs, blending well.
3. In another bowl mix together baking soda, oat bran, bran cereal, and flour.
4. Add to first mixture alternately with buttermilk.
5. Oil muffin tins; fill ⅔ full and bake for 30 minutes, until tops are golden brown.

Yields: 2 dozen muffins.

Baked Blueberry French Bread

This is a baked version of French toast using French bread. You will need to begin this recipe a few hours ahead of serving time, or you can start it the night before.

Ingredients:

    16 oz. French bread
    4 eggs
    ½ c. milk
    ¼ tsp. baking powder
    1 tsp. vanilla extract
    2½ c. blueberries, frozen or fresh
    ½ c. sugar
    1 tsp. ground cinnamon
    1 tsp. cornstarch
    2 Tbs. butter, melted
    ¼ c. confectioners' sugar

Directions:

1. Slice bread on diagonal to create eight ¾-inch-thick pieces, heels removed.
2. Arrange bread slices in 10 x 15-inch baking dish.
3. In medium bowl whip together eggs, milk, baking powder, and vanilla.
4. Slowly pour mixture over bread, turning each slice to coat completely.
5. Cover dish with plastic wrap, and refrigerate for at least 1 hour but preferably overnight.
6. Preheat oven to 425 degrees F.
7. Coat another 10 x 15-inch baking dish with nonstick cooking spray.
8. Sprinkle blueberries over bottom of pan.
9. Mix together sugar, cinnamon, and cornstarch; pour evenly over top of berries.
10. Tightly wedge bread slices over blueberries, wettest side up; brush bread with melted butter.

11. Bake in center of oven for 20 to 25 minutes or until golden brown.
12. To serve, place toast berry side down on warmed plates.
13. Stir remaining berry mixture in baking dish, then scoop over toast.
14. Sprinkle with confectioners' sugar.
15. Note: This has lots of blueberries in it. When fresh berries are very sweet, reduce amount of sugar.

Yields: 8 servings.

Blueberry Fritters

My mom used to make us warm apple fritters for breakfast as a special treat when I was a child. This is an alternate version and makes a great special, easy-to-make breakfast. These are delicious served warm.

Ingredients:
    1½ c. all-purpose flour
    ¾   c. sugar
    3   tsp. baking powder
    ¾   c. fresh blueberries
    1   egg, beaten
    1   c. milk
         vegetable oil for deep frying
         sugar, powdered sugar, or cinnamon sugar

Directions:
    1. Preheat deep oil to 375 degrees F.
    2. Sift together flour, sugar, and baking powder; add berries.
    3. Beat egg and milk together; add to dry mixture, mixing just until moistened.
    4. Drop batter by tablespoonfuls into hot oil.
    5. Fry until golden brown, 3 to 4 minutes, turning once; drain on paper towels.
    6. Roll in sugar, powdered sugar, or cinnamon sugar.

Blueberry Skillet Soufflé

This nice soufflé makes a great breakfast dish.

Ingredients:

- 2 pt. fresh blueberries, divided
- ⅓ c. blueberry preserves (recipe page 196)
- 1 Tbs. framboise (raspberry-flavored liqueur)
- 2 Tbs. unsalted butter (no substitutions)
- 8 lg. egg whites
- ¼ tsp. cream of tartar
- ¼ tsp. salt
- ¼ c. plus 2 Tbs. sugar, divided

Directions:

1. Preheat oven to 375 degrees F.
2. Mash 1 cup blueberries and blueberry preserves with potato masher in bowl; stir in framboise.
3. Melt butter in deep 10- or 11-inch skillet over low heat.
4. Meanwhile, beat egg whites, cream of tartar, and salt to soft peaks in large mixer bowl.
5. Gradually beat in ¼ cup sugar; beat to stiff peaks.
6. Fold blueberry mixture into white's ⅓ at a time, just until blended.
7. Increase heat under skillet to medium-low.
8. Pour mixture into skillet, gently spreading to sides and mounding in center; cook 2 minutes.
9. Transfer skillet to oven and bake soufflé 15 minutes, until set.
10. Add remaining blueberries to bowl.
11. Toss with remaining 2 tablespoons sugar.
12. Serve soufflé immediately, topped with berries.

Blueberry Delights Cookbook

A Collection of Blueberry Recipes
Cookbook Delights Series-Book 2

Cakes

Table of Contents

Did You Know? . . . .

Did you know that blueberries, especially wild species, contain anthocyanins, other antioxidant pigments and other phytochemicals which may have a role in reducing the risks of some diseases, including cancers?

Blueberry Upside-Down Cake

This cake is absolutely delicious when served warm and topped with sweetened whipped cream.

Ingredients:

- 2 c. fresh blueberries
- 1½ c. sugar, divided
- 2 c. plus 2 Tbs. all-purpose flour, divided
- 3 Tbs. freshly grated lemon rind
- ½ c. butter, softened
- 3 eggs
- 1 tsp. pure vanilla extract
- ¼ tsp. almond extract
- 4 tsp. baking powder
- ¼ tsp. salt
- ¾ c. whole milk
- ½ c. toasted slivered almonds
- Sweetened Whipped Cream (recipe page 238)

Directions:

1. Preheat oven to 350 degrees F.
2. Mix blueberries, ½ cup sugar, 2 tablespoons flour, and lemon rind; spread evenly into greased and floured 9-inch spring form pan.
3. Beat butter and remaining 1 cup sugar until fluffy; beat in eggs and extracts.
4. Mix remaining 2 cups flour, baking powder, and salt; beat into creamy mixture alternately with milk until just moistened.
5. Pour over blueberries and spread evenly.
6. Bake 60 to 70 minutes or until wooden pick inserted in center comes out clean.
7. Let sit in pan about 5 minutes, then place serving plate over top of pan; carefully invert cake and plate together.
8. Remove sides from cake pan.
9. Serve warm, topped with almonds.
10. Garnish with whipped cream as desired.
11. Refrigerate leftovers.

Sour Cream Blueberry Cake

This is a simple, hearty cake similar to a pound cake, which my husband always enjoys. Try it with or without frosting.

Ingredients:

    2   c. sifted all-purpose flour
    1   tsp. baking soda
    ½   tsp. salt
    ½   c. butter, softened
    1   c. sugar
    3   eggs
    1   c. sour cream
    1   tsp. vanilla extract
    1¼ c. blueberries
    ½   c. brown sugar, firmly packed
    ¾   c. chopped hazelnuts
    ½   tsp. ground cinnamon

Directions:

1. Preheat oven to 350 degrees F.
2. Sift together flour, baking soda, and salt; set aside.
3. Cream butter, sugar, eggs, sour cream, and vanilla together until light and smooth.
4. Add dry ingredients, blending well, then gently fold in blueberries.
5. Spread ½ of batter into greased 13 x 9 x 2-inch baking dish.
6. Mix together brown sugar, nuts, and cinnamon.
7. Sprinkle mixture over top of batter, then top with remaining batter.
8. Bake 40 minutes or until wooden pick inserted near center comes out clean.
9. Cool before cutting into squares and serving.

Blueberry Crunch Coffee Ring

This makes a great-tasting dessert or breakfast.

Ingredients for walnut streusel:

¾ c. finely chopped walnuts, divided
½ c. brown sugar, firmly packed
2 Tbs. all-purpose flour
2 tsp. ground cinnamon
2 Tbs. butter, melted

Ingredients for cake:

1½ c. all-purpose flour
¾ c. sugar
1 Tbs. baking powder
½ tsp. salt
¼ tsp. ground nutmeg
⅓ c. butter, firm
1 c. blueberries
1 egg
½ c. milk
1 tsp. vanilla extract
   confectioners' sugar

Directions:

1. Preheat oven to 350 degrees F.
2. Mix ½ cup chopped walnuts, brown sugar, flour, and cinnamon with 2 tablespoons melted butter.
3. Pat about ½ the streusel into greased and flour-dusted 9-inch tube pan or layer cake pan with removable bottom; set aside.
4. In large bowl stir together flour, sugar, baking powder, salt, and nutmeg.
5. Using pastry blender or 2 knives, cut in butter until mixture resembles coarse crumbs.

6. Gently stir in blueberries.
7. Beat egg lightly with milk and vanilla; stir into berry mixture just until combined.
8. Spread half the batter in streusel-lined pan; sprinkle with remaining streusel then with remaining batter.
9. Bake until wooden pick inserted in center comes out clean, 45 to 60 minutes.
10. Let cool in pan for 20 minutes, then remove pan sides.
11. Dust with confectioners' sugar.
12. Serve warm or cool.

Blueberry Cheesecake

This is an easy-to-make version of cheesecake that is very tasty.

Ingredients:

1   graham cracker crust (recipe page 225)
2   pkg. cream cheese (8 oz. each), softened
¾   c. sugar
¼   tsp. vanilla extract
2   eggs
1½ c. blueberries, divided

Directions:

1. Preheat oven to 350 degrees F.
2. Mix cream cheese, sugar, and vanilla until smooth and creamy.
3. Add eggs and mix well, then pour into pie crust.
4. Spoon ¼ to ⅓ cup blueberries on top.
5. Gently swirl with toothpick.
6. Bake for 40 minutes or until center is set.
7. Cool to room temperature, then refrigerate.
8. Serve topped with remaining blueberries.

Blueberry Molasses Cake

If you enjoy the flavor of molasses, you will certainly enjoy this cake. The blueberries add extra flavor, color, and nutrition.

Ingredients:

- 1 c. sugar
- 1 c. oil
- 4 eggs
- 2 c. molasses
- 4 c. all-purpose flour
- 2 tsp. salt
- 2 tsp. ground cinnamon
- 1 tsp. ground ginger
- 1 tsp. ground allspice
- ½ tsp. ground cloves
- 2 tsp. baking soda
- 1 c. hot water
- 3 c. blueberries, fresh or frozen

Directions:

1. Preheat oven to 325 degrees F.
2. In large bowl whip together sugar, oil, eggs, and molasses.
3. In separate bowl sift together flour, salt, and spices.
4. Add dry ingredients to molasses mixture alternately with baking soda dissolved in hot water.
5. Add blueberries and pour into greased 12 x 16-inch sheet pan.
6. Bake for 1 hour or until cake tests done.

Yields: 12 servings.

Blueberry Carrot Cake

A dollop of whipped cream and a sprinkle of fresh blueberries on top of a slice of this delightfully moist cake is quite a treat.

Ingredients:

- 1   c. oil
- 1   c. brown sugar, firmly packed
- 1   tsp. vanilla extract
- 1   c. chunky applesauce
- 2   eggs
- 2½ c. all-purpose flour
- 2   tsp. baking soda
- 2   tsp. ground cinnamon
- ½   tsp. salt
- 2   c. shredded carrots
- ½   c. chopped walnuts
- 1   c. fresh blueberries

Directions:

1. Preheat oven to 350 degrees F.
2. Grease 12-cup fluted tube pan.
3. In large bowl combine oil, brown sugar, vanilla, applesauce, and eggs; mix well.
4. Stir in flour, baking soda, cinnamon, and salt; mix well.
5. Stir in carrots and walnuts, and then gently stir in blueberries.
6. Pour into prepared pan, and bake 50 to 60 minutes or until wooden pick inserted in center comes out clean.
7. Cool 15 minutes, then invert onto serving plate and cool completely.
8. Serve with whipped cream and fresh blueberries.

Yields: 16 servings.

Blueberry and Orange Layer Cake

This elegant cake has a soft, warm texture and a wonderful flavor.

Ingredients for cake:

2½ c. cake flour
2   tsp. baking powder
½   tsp. salt
½   c. plus 2 Tbs. unsalted butter, room temperature
1½ c. sugar
3   Tbs. frozen orange juice concentrate, thawed
1½ tsp. grated orange peel
1   tsp. vanilla extract
4   lg. eggs
1   c. whole milk

Ingredients for filling:

2½ pt. fresh blueberries
2   Tbs. sugar
1   tsp. fresh lemon juice

Ingredients for frosting:

8   oz. cream cheese, room temperature
½   c. unsalted butter, room temperature
3¼ c. confectioners' sugar
2   Tbs. frozen orange juice concentrate, thawed
1   tsp. grated orange peel
½   tsp. vanilla extract
2½ pt. fresh blueberries for garnish
    orange peel strips for garnish

Directions for cake:

1. Preheat oven to 350 degrees F.
2. Butter and flour two 9-inches round cake pans with 1½-inch-high sides; line bottoms with rounds of parchment paper.
3. Sift flour, baking powder, and salt into medium bowl; set aside.
4. In large bowl beat butter until fluffy; gradually add sugar, beating until blended.
5. Beat in concentrate, peel, and vanilla.
6. Beat in eggs one at a time, beating well after each addition.
7. Beat in flour mixture in 4 additions alternating with milk in 3 additions.
8. Divide batter between prepared pans.
9. Bake cakes until tester inserted into center comes out clean, about 30 minutes; cool in pans on rack.

Directions for filling:

1. Combine berries, sugar, and lemon juice in heavy small saucepan.
2. Bring to boil over high heat, stirring until sugar dissolves.
3. Boil until mixture is reduced to ¾ cup, stirring occasionally and mashing berries coarsely with fork, about 8 minutes.
4. Chill filling uncovered until cold, about 30 minutes.

Directions for frosting:

1. Beat cream cheese and butter in bowl to blend.
2. Beat in confectioners' sugar in 4 additions, and then beat in orange concentrate, peel, and vanilla.
3. Chill until firm but spreadable, about 30 minutes.

Directions for assembly:

1. Cut around cakes to loosen, turn cakes out, and peel off parchment.
2. Place 1 layer, flat side up, on platter.
3. Spread filling to within ½ inch of edges; chill 5 minutes.
4. Top with second layer, flat side down.
5. Spread ½ cup frosting thinly all over cake to seal.
6. Spread remaining frosting over cake.
7. Spread blueberries over top of cake, and garnish with strips of orange peel.
8. Can be made 1 day ahead; chill.
9. Serve at room temperature.

Yields: 10 to 12 servings.

Very Blueberry Cake

This blueberry cake can be used either as a dessert, for brunch, or for breakfast. The glaze is an added sweet touch.

Ingredients for cake:

1   c. butter, softened
1½ c. sugar
4   eggs
1   tsp. vanilla extract
1   tsp. almond extract
3   c. all-purpose flour
½   tsp. baking powder

Ingredients for filling:

1   Tbs. all-purpose flour
2   tsp. cornstarch

1   tsp. quick-cooking tapioca
4   c. fresh or frozen blueberries, divided
1   tsp. grated lemon rind

Ingredients for glaze:

1   c. confectioners' sugar
2   Tbs. milk
1   tsp. lemon juice

Directions for cake:

1. Butter 15 x 10 x 1-inch baking pan.
2. In mixing bowl cream butter and sugar.
3. Beat in eggs one at a time; add extracts.
4. Combine flour and baking powder; add to creamed mixture and mix well.
5. Spread ⅔ of batter in prepared pan.

Directions for filling:

1. Preheat oven to 350 degrees F.
2. Combine flour, cornstarch, and tapioca in large bowl.
3. Add ½ cup blueberries; mash with fork and stir well.
4. Add lemon peel and remaining berries; toss to coat.
5. Pour evenly over batter in pan.
6. Drop remaining batter by rounded tablespoonfuls over filling.
7. Bake for 40 minutes or until golden brown.

Directions for glaze:

1. Combine glaze ingredients; drizzle over warm cake.

Yields: 20 servings.

Blueberry-Peach Pound Cake

This is a delicious version of pound cake.

Ingredients:

½   c. butter, softened
1¼ c. sugar
3   eggs
¼   c. milk
2½ c. cake flour
2   tsp. baking powder
¼   tsp. salt
2¼ c. fresh peaches, peeled, cut in ½-inch pieces
2   c. blueberries, fresh or frozen
     confectioner's sugar (optional)

Directions:

1. Preheat oven to 350 degrees F.
2. In mixing bowl, cream butter and sugar.
3. Beat in eggs one at a time, mixing well after each addition.
4. Beat in milk.
5. Combine flour, baking powder, and salt; add to creamed mixture.
6. Stir in peaches and blueberries.
7. Pour into greased and floured 10-inch fluted tube pan.
8. Bake 60 to 70 minutes or until wooden pick inserted near center comes out clean.
9. Cool in pan for 15 minutes, and then remove to wire rack to cool completely.
10. Dust with confectioner's sugar if desired.

Yields: 10 to 12 servings.

Old-Fashioned Apple Blueberry Cake

Blueberries and apples make great companions in this cake. Since you can use frozen blueberries and apples are available year round, you can enjoy this delicious cake any time.

Ingredients:

½   c. unsalted butter
¼   c. whipping cream
1¼ c. sugar
3   eggs
2⅓ c. all-purpose flour
2   tsp. baking powder
1   tsp. salt
2   c. peeled, cored, coarsely chopped Granny Smith apples
2   c. frozen blueberries
     Sweetened Whipped Cream (recipe page 238)

Directions:

1. Preheat oven to 350 degrees F.
2. In 1-quart saucepan melt butter in cream over low heat, stirring occasionally; set aside.
3. In large mixing bowl combine sugar and eggs; beat with electric mixer on medium speed, scraping bowl often, until well mixed.
4. Add butter mixture, flour, baking powder, and salt; continue beating, scraping bowl often, until smooth.
5. By hand, stir in apples and blueberries.
6. Spread into greased and floured 13 x 9 x 2-inch baking pan.
7. Bake 45 to 55 minutes or until wooden pick inserted in center comes out clean.
8. Serve warm with whipped cream.

Yields: 15 servings.

Lemon Tea Cake with Blueberry Red Wine Sauce

This moist, flavorful cake can be made a day ahead. Make sure to use a good wine for best flavor. The sauce can also be used over ice cream or pork.

Ingredients for sauce:

½ c. water
½ c. sugar
½ c. dry red wine
3 Tbs. freshly squeezed lemon juice
1½ Tbs. cornstarch
1 c. fresh blueberries
¼ tsp. ground cinnamon
⅛ tsp. ground nutmeg

Ingredients for cake:

½ c. unsalted butter, room temperature
1 c. sugar
3 lg. eggs
2 Tbs. grated lemon peel
2 Tbs. fresh lemon juice
1 tsp. vanilla extract
1½ c. sifted cake flour
½ tsp. baking powder
¼ tsp. baking soda
¼ tsp. salt
½ c. sour cream
   nonstick vegetable oil spray

Directions for sauce:

1. Stir water, sugar, wine, lemon juice, and cornstarch in medium saucepan over medium heat until cornstarch dissolves and mixture boils.

2. Add blueberries.
3. Boil until sauce thickens enough to coat back of spoon, stirring constantly, about 5 minutes.
4. Cool 10 minutes.
5. Stir in spices; cool.

Directions for cake:

1. Preheat oven to 325 degrees F.
2. Spray 8-inch square glass baking dish with nonstick vegetable oil spray.
3. Line bottom of baking dish with parchment paper; spray parchment with vegetable oil spray.
4. Dust dish and parchment with flour.
5. Beat butter and sugar in large bowl until fluffy.
6. Beat in eggs one at a time.
7. Beat in grated lemon peel, lemon juice, and vanilla.
8. Sift flour, baking powder, baking soda, and salt into medium bowl.
9. Mix dry ingredients into butter mixture alternately with sour cream.
10. Pour batter into prepared baking pan.
11. Bake until tester inserted into center comes out clean, about 45 minutes.
12. Cool cake on rack 10 minutes.
13. Cut around sides of cake, turn out onto rack, and peel off paper.
14. Turn cake over; cool completely.
15. Sauce and cake can be prepared 1 day ahead. Refrigerate sauce. Wrap cake in aluminum foil, and store at room temperature.
16. When ready to serve, cut cake into triangles and arrange on plates; spoon sauce over.

Yields: 6 servings.

Blueberry Pound Cake

My husband loves pound cake, and this excellent pound cake has the added treat of blueberries.

Ingredients:

- 1 c. butter, softened
- 2 c. sugar
- 4 eggs
- 1 tsp. vanilla extract
- 3 c. all-purpose flour, divided
- ¼ tsp. salt
- 1 tsp. baking powder
- 2 c. blueberries

Directions:

1. Preheat oven to 325 degrees F.
2. Cream butter and sugar.
3. Add eggs one at a time; beat well until light and fluffy, then add vanilla.
4. Sift 2 cups flour, salt, and baking powder together.
5. Add sifted ingredients to creamed mixture and beat.
6. Dredge berries in remaining flour.
7. Fold blueberry mixture gently into creamed mixture.
8. Pour into 10-inch tube or Bundt pan which has been buttered and coated with sugar.
9. Bake for 1 hour and 15 minutes.

Did You Know?....

Did you know that early American colonists made grey paint by boiling blueberries in milk?

Blueberry Delights Cookbook
A Collection of Blueberry Recipes
Cookbook Delights Series-Book 2

Candies

Table of Contents

Page

Did You Know?....

Did you know that the total production of wild blueberries in North America averages over 120 million pounds annually?

Blueberry Cheesecake Fudge

This is a fun variation on the traditional Christmas fudge.

Ingredients:

⅔ c. evaporated milk

2½ c. sugar

5 oz. marshmallow cream

¼ c. butter

3 oz. cream cheese, room temperature

12 oz. white chocolate chips

1½ c. dried blueberries (recipe page 253)

1 tsp. vanilla extract

Directions:

1. Heat milk over medium heat until warm; add sugar.
2. Over medium heat bring mixture to rolling boil, stirring constantly with wooden spoon.
3. Remove from heat; add marshmallow cream and butter.
4. Bring back to rolling boil for 5½ minutes by the clock; start timing once rolling boil resumes.
5. Cut cream cheese into small pieces to allow easy melting, and add to boiling mixture about 1 minute before end of boil.
6. If brown flakes appear in mixture, turn down heat a little.
7. Remove from heat, and add white chocolate chips and blueberries.
8. Stir until creamy and all chips are melted.
9. Stir in vanilla extract.
10. Mix thoroughly and pour into lightly buttered 9 x 9-inch baking pan.

11. Cool on wire rack, and then cut into squares before serving.
12. May be stored in airtight container in refrigerator for up to 3 weeks or in freezer up to 3 months.

Yields: 16 to 20 pieces.

Red, White, and Blueberry Bark

This is a simple, refreshing candy. The dried blueberries and cranberries are a tart contrast to the sweet chocolate. Other dried fruits may also be substituted in this recipe.

Ingredients:

12 oz. white chocolate, finely chopped
1   c. dried blueberries (recipe page 253)
1   c. dried cranberries

Directions:

1. Line baking sheet with aluminum foil.
2. Melt chocolate.
3. Pour onto baking sheet, and tilt sheet to spread chocolate in smooth, thin layer. (If necessary, use offset spatula or knife to achieve desired thinness.)
4. While chocolate is still wet, sprinkle dried blueberries and cranberries over the top, pressing gently to embed them in chocolate.
5. Place baking sheet in refrigerator to set chocolate.
6. When firm, break bark into irregular-size pieces.
7. Refrigerate until ready to serve.

Blueberry Cream Fudge

Blueberry cream fudge is a great treat. Enjoy this colorful, creamy fudge.

Ingredients:

- 2 c. sugar
- 1 c. light cream
- 1 Tbs. light corn syrup
- ½ tsp. salt
- 1 Tbs. butter
- 2 tsp. pure vanilla extract
- ¾ c. blueberries

Directions:

1. In heavy 2-quart saucepan combine sugar, cream, corn syrup, and salt.
2. Bring to boil over moderate heat, stirring constantly.
3. Cook to soft-ball stage (238 degrees F.).
4. Remove from heat, and cool to 110 degrees F. or to lukewarm; do not stir.
5. Add butter and vanilla; beat until mixture becomes very thick and loses its gloss.
6. Stir in blueberries, and spread in 8 x 8-inch buttered pan.
7. Score squares while fudge is still warm.
8. When cooled, cut into squares to serve.

Did You Know?....

Did you know that Maine produces 25 percent of all blueberries in North America, making it the largest producer in the world?

Blueberry Nuggets

Fruit and nut nugget candy rolled in confectioners' sugar is a very popular candy in the Northwest. This candy can be made at home as a real treat. This was a favorite of one of my daughters.

Ingredients:

    2   env. unflavored gelatin
    1½ c. blueberry purée, divided
    2   c. sugar
    1   c. chopped walnuts
    ¼   tsp. almond extract
        confectioners' sugar

Directions:

1. Sprinkle gelatin over ½ cup of blueberry purée; set aside and let stand.
2. Combine remaining blueberry purée and sugar in saucepan; bring to a boil over moderate heat, stirring constantly.
3. Add softened gelatin mixture and continue stirring; bring to rolling boil, and cook for 15 to 20 minutes longer.
4. Stir in nuts and almond extract.
5. Pour into buttered 8 x 8-inch pan.
6. Cool to room temperature; refrigerate overnight.
7. Cut into 1 x 1-inch pieces.
8. Carefully invert onto firm surface to remove from pan; roll each piece in confectioners' sugar.
9. Allow to stand 2 to 3 days before serving.

Did You Know? . . . .

Did you know that highbush blueberries can produce for 40 to 50 years?

Double Berry Truffles

The blueberry preserves and dried strawberries give these truffles a burst of berry flavor. You can omit the bright blue food coloring, but if you do, the filling will be a dull purple-gray. Any dried berry may be substituted for the dried strawberries.

Ingredients:

1	lb. white chocolate, divided
8	oz. cream cheese, softened, divided
¾	c. vanilla wafer cookie crumbs
½	c. blueberry preserves (recipe page 196)
1	tsp. vanilla extract
3-4	drops blue food coloring
30	pieces freeze-dried strawberries

Directions:

1. Melt 6 ounces white chocolate (about 1 cup of chip-size pieces) in microwave or over double boiler, and allow cooling slightly.
2. Place softened cream cheese in mixing bowl, and beat on medium-high until smooth and creamy.
3. Add melted chocolate and beat until smooth.
4. Stir in cookie crumbs, preserves, vanilla, and food coloring.
5. Cover with plastic wrap, and chill in refrigerator for about 1 hour, until firm enough to roll.
6. Shape mixture into small balls; place on baking sheet covered with aluminum foil.
7. Refrigerate until balls are firm, about 1 hour.
8. Melt remaining 10 ounces of chocolate.
9. Dip truffles in chocolate, using dipping tools or two forks.

10. Place chocolate-coated truffles back on baking sheet, and while chocolate is still wet, top with piece of dried strawberry.
11. Return truffles to refrigerator to set chocolate.
12. Serve straight from refrigerator.

Blueberry Divinity

These are wonderful, easy-to-make treats that are enjoyable for all. The blue juice adds an attractive color to the divinity.

Ingredients:

2 c. sugar
½ c. blueberry juice (recipe page 252)
½ tsp. salt
1 pt. marshmallow cream
½ c. chopped nuts
1 tsp. vanilla extract

Directions:

1. In medium saucepan boil together sugar, juice, and salt until it forms hard ball in cool water.
2. Place marshmallow cream in mixing bowl; beat in hot syrup.
3. Continue beating until slightly stiff and will hold a peak; fold in nuts and vanilla.
4. Drop from spoon onto wax paper; allow to sit until firm.
5. May be kept in airtight container for up to 3 weeks or freeze for up to 3 months.

Easy Chocolate and Blueberry Truffles

These are rich, delicious, melt-in-your-mouth candies. Make lots, as they do go fast!

Ingredients:

  8 oz. semisweet chocolate, coarsely chopped
  4 oz. unsweetened chocolate
  8 Tbs. unsalted butter
  1 can sweetened condensed milk (14 oz.)
  6 Tbs. orange-flavored liqueur
  ½ tsp. finely grated orange zest
  ½ c. blueberry fruit leather (recipe page 246) or dried berries, finely chopped
  1 c. finely chopped toasted almonds
  ½ c. instant chocolate drink powder

Directions:

1. Heat both chocolates, butter, and milk in saucepan until chocolates and butter are partially melted.
2. Remove from heat, and continue to stir until completely melted.
3. Whisk in liqueur and orange zest until creamy and smooth; stir in blueberry bits.
4. Transfer to bowl, and let stand until firm enough to hold its shape, about 2 hours.
5. Using a tablespoon, mold chocolate into balls, 1 level tablespoon at a time; place on cookie sheet lined with buttered parchment paper.
6. Place chopped almonds and chocolate powder in small bowl; mix well.
7. Working with one at a time, drop truffles into bowl with greased fingertips.
8. Shake bowl back and forth so truffles are completely coated.

9. Return to parchment paper to set for about 1 hour before serving.
10. Can be refrigerated in airtight container up to 5 days or frozen up to 1 month before serving; let stand at room temperature to soften slightly.

Yields: 3 dozen balls.

White Chocolate Berry Clusters

This is a quick and easy fruit and nut cluster with coconut.

Ingredients:

1 lb. white chocolate, melting type
1 c. dried blueberries (recipe page 253)
¾ c. unsweetened natural coconut
½ c. chopped nuts

Directions:

1. Melt chocolate in pan over hot water. (Do not let water come to a boil.)
2. When chocolate is completely melted, remove from heat.
3. Stir in remaining ingredients immediately.
4. Place by teaspoonfuls onto wax paper.
5. Let cool completely before removing.

Yields: 24 clusters (2 inches each).

Did You Know? . . . .

Did you know that the Canadian blueberry is one of the sweetest blueberries known?

Chocolate-Covered Blueberries

This is a delicious and wonderful way to eat your fruit and have some chocolate, too!

Ingredients:

    1 c. semisweet chocolate chips
    1 Tbs. unsalted butter
    2 c. fresh blueberries, rinsed, dried

Directions:

1. Melt chocolate in glass bowl in microwave or in metal bowl set over pan of simmering water.
2. Stir frequently until melted and smooth; remove from heat and stir in butter until melted.
3. Cool mixture somewhat; add blueberries to chocolate, stirring gently to coat.
4. Quickly spoon small clumps of candy mixture onto wax paper-lined baking sheet.
5. Refrigerate until firm, about 10 minutes, before serving.
6. May be stored in cool place in airtight container for 2 to 3 days.
7. Note: These also may be made with chopped blueberry fruit leather in place of fresh berries. They will store up to 1 month in airtight container.

Yields: 2½ dozen pieces.

Did You Know? . . . .

Did you know that blueberries also contain a yellow pigment, which in an alkaline environment, such as a batter with too much baking soda, may give it a greenish-blue color?

Blueberry Nut Candy with Chocolate

This is a delicious and chewy chocolate candy with the zing of blueberry flavor.

Ingredients:

½ c. butter
1 can sweetened condensed milk (14 oz.)
1 pkg. chocolate chips (12 oz.)
1 pkg. butterscotch chips (6 oz.)
½ c. finely chopped pecans
½ c. finely chopped blueberry fruit leather (recipe page 240)
1 pkg. miniature marshmallows (10½ oz.)
1 tsp. vanilla extract

Directions:

1. In saucepan combine butter and condensed milk; bring to a boil then remove from heat.
2. Stir in chocolate chips and butterscotch chips, and stir until melted.
3. Stir in nuts, blueberry bits, marshmallows, and vanilla.
4. Drop by spoonfuls onto wax paper.
5. Let sit until firm, then they may be wrapped or stored in airtight container in refrigerator for up to 3 weeks or freeze for up to 3 months.

Yields: 2 to 2½ dozen pieces.

Did You Know? . . . .

Did you know that Nova Scotia is the largest processor of wild blueberries in the world?

Blueberry Nut Fudge

My children love this fudge, and it is a breeze to make.

Ingredients:

- 4 c. brown sugar, firmly packed
- 8 oz. evaporated milk
- 3 Tbs. butter
- ⅓ c. corn syrup
- 2 Tbs. blueberry juice (recipe page 252)
- ¾ c. chopped walnuts
- ½ c. dried blueberries (recipe page 253)

Directions:

1. Over medium-high heat, bring sugar, milk, butter, syrup, and blueberry juice to full boil; boil exactly 4 minutes.
2. Remove from heat, and beat with electric mixer for 10 minutes; stir in nuts and blueberries.
3. Spread into greased 8 x 8-inch pan; cut into squares before it cools completely.
4. Turn out onto board, wrap individually if desired, and store in airtight container.
5. This fudge freezes well for up to 3 months.

Did You Know? . . . .

Did you know that Chile is the biggest blueberry producer in South America and the largest exporter to the northern hemisphere?

Blueberry Delights Cookbook

A Collection of Blueberry Recipes
Cookbook Delights Series-Book 2

Cookies

Table of Contents

Did You Know? . . . .

Did you know that blueberries were once called "star berries"? That is because of the star-shaped formation on their skin left from the flower that formed the fruit.

Frosty Blueberry Squares

This is a refreshing blueberry dessert that can be made ahead and taken out in a hurry for unexpected company.

Ingredients for crust:

- 1   c. all-purpose flour
- ¾ c. chopped hazelnuts
- ½ c. butter, melted
- ¼ c. brown sugar, firmly packed

Ingredients for filling:

- 2   c. whipping cream, divided
- 2½ c. blueberries, fresh or frozen
- 1   c. sugar
- 2   Tbs. lemon juice

Directions for crust:

1. Preheat oven to 350 degrees F.
2. In medium bowl combine flour, nuts, butter, and brown sugar to make crumb mixture.
3. Spread evenly into greased shallow baking pan.
4. Bake for 10 minutes, stir, and continue baking for another 10 minutes.
5. Sprinkle ⅔ of baked crumbs into 13 x 9 x 2-inch baking pan; reserve remaining crumbs for topping.

Directions for filling:

1. In large mixing bowl combine 1 cup whipping cream, blueberries, sugar, and lemon juice.
2. Beat with electric mixer on high speed about 10 minutes or until stiff peaks form.
3. In small mixing bowl beat remaining 1 cup whipping cream into stiff peaks.

4. Fold into blueberry mixture and spoon evenly over crumbs in baking pan.
5. Sprinkle remaining crumbs on top.
6. Cover and freeze until firm and ready to serve.

Yields: 12 to 14 servings.

Blueberry Bars

These delicious bars are not only easy to make, but they also freeze well. You can make them ahead to have on hand for lunchbox treats.

Ingredients:

¾ c. butter, softened
1 c. brown sugar, firmly packed
1½ c. all-purpose flour
½ tsp. salt
½ tsp. baking soda
1½ c. rolled oats
9 oz. blueberry preserves (recipe page 196)

Directions:

1. Preheat oven to 400 degrees F.
2. In medium bowl cream together butter and sugar.
3. Add dry ingredients, and stir with fork to consistency of crumbs.
4. Pat half of crumb mixture into buttered 13 x 9 x 2-inch pan.
5. Spread with preserves, and sprinkle with remaining crumb mixture.
6. Bake for 25 minutes.
7. Remove from oven and cool on wire rack; cut into squares before serving.

Yields: 12 to 14 servings.

Blueberry Pinwheels

These make attractive, colored pinwheels that taste great. Adding grated orange peel makes it an extra-tasty treat.

Ingredients:

    1   c. blueberry jelly (recipe page 205)
    1   Tbs. cornstarch
    ½   c. butter, softened
    ¾   c. sugar
    1   egg
    1¾ c. all-purpose flour
    1   tsp. baking powder
    ¼   tsp. ground allspice
    1   tsp. finely grated fresh orange peel

Directions:

1. Combine blueberry jelly and cornstarch in small saucepan; bring to a boil over moderate heat, stirring constantly.
2. Remove from heat and refrigerate until cooled.
3. Cream butter and sugar; add egg and beat until fluffy.
4. Stir in flour, baking powder, and allspice, blending well; stir in grated orange peel.
5. Cover with plastic wrap, and chill in refrigerator for at least 1 hour.
6. On lightly floured surface, roll out chilled dough into 16 x 8-inch rectangle.
7. Spread cooled blueberry filling on dough to within ½ inch of edges.
8. Starting with long edge, roll up.
9. Cut in half, wrap each piece in plastic, and refrigerate for 2 hours.
10. Preheat oven to 375 degrees F.

11. With sharp knife, cut cookies about ½ inch thick, and place on greased cookie sheet, 2 inches apart.
12. Bake for 10 to 12 minutes.
13. Remove from oven, and gently lift with spatula onto wire rack to cool.

Yields: 30 cookies.

Blueberry Oatmeal Bars

Oatmeal and blueberries make a great taste combination, and the coconut adds texture and flavor.

Ingredients:
    1¼ c. all-purpose flour
    1½ c. quick-cooking oats
    ½   c. sugar
    ½   tsp. baking soda
    ⅓   c. butter, melted
    2   tsp. pure vanilla extract
    1   c. shredded coconut
        blueberry jam (recipe page 194)

Directions:
1. Preheat oven to 350 degrees F.
2. Combine flour, oats, sugar, soda, butter, and vanilla to make crumb mixture.
3. Reserve 1 cup of mixture; press remaining amount onto bottom of greased 13 x 9 x 2-inch baking pan.
4. Spread blueberry jam onto this mixture; sprinkle coconut and reserved crumb mixture over top.
5. Bake for about 25 minutes.
6. Cool completely before cutting into bars.

Yields: 2 dozen bars.

Blueberry Shortbread Bars

These are very tasty blueberry bars that can be made year round with your favorite blueberry jam.

Ingredients for bottom layer:

1½ c. all-purpose flour
½ c. sugar
½ c. butter
¾ c. blueberry jam (recipe page 194)

Ingredients for top layer:

2 Tbs. all-purpose flour
¼ tsp. salt
¼ tsp. baking soda
2 eggs, lightly beaten
½ c. brown sugar, firmly packed
1 tsp. pure vanilla extract
1¼ c. chopped walnuts

Directions for bottom layer:

1. Preheat oven to 350 degrees F.
2. In medium bowl combine flour with sugar; cut in butter until mixture resembles fine crumbs.
3. Press into bottom of greased 9 x 9-inch baking pan.
4. Bake for 20 minutes; remove from oven and let cool in pan. (Leave oven on.)
5. Spread blueberry jam over crust.

Directions for top layer:

1. Mix flour, salt, and baking soda.
2. Combine eggs, brown sugar, and vanilla; stir in flour mixture.
3. Fold in walnuts and spoon over jam layer.

4. Return to oven and bake 20 minutes longer.
5. Cool in pan, dust with confectioners' sugar if desired, and cut into bars.

Yields: 20 servings.

Blueberry Drop Cookies

These cookies take a little extra time since the dough is chilled for four hours.

Ingredients:

½   c. butter, softened
1   c. sugar
1   egg
¼   c. milk
1   tsp. almond extract
1½ tsp. lemon zest
2   c. all-purpose flour
2   tsp. baking powder
½   tsp. salt
1½ c. blueberries

Directions:

1. In large bowl cream butter, sugar, egg, milk, almond extract, and lemon zest; mix well.
2. Slowly add in flour, baking powder, and salt.
3. Fold in blueberries and mix until well blended.
4. Cover and chill for about 4 hours.
5. Preheat oven to 375 degrees F.
6. Drop dough by teaspoonfuls onto ungreased cookie sheets, about 1½ inch apart.
7. Bake 12 to 15 minutes or until lightly browned.
8. Remove to wire rack to cool.

Yields: About 3 dozen.

Blueberry Thumbprint Cookies

When I was a child, my mom made thumbprint cookies, which I really enjoyed. This is a great-tasting version using your favorite blueberry jam.

Ingredients:

- 1 c. butter, softened
- 1 c. brown sugar, firmly packed
- 2 eggs, separated
- 2 c. all-purpose flour
- 1 c. ground walnuts
- 1 c. blueberry jam (recipe page 194)

Directions:

1. In large bowl cream butter and sugar; add egg yolks and mix until smooth.
2. Combine with flour and refrigerate until firm.
3. Preheat oven to 325 degrees F.
4. Remove dough from refrigerator and form into 1-inch balls.
5. Lightly beat egg whites with fork until thin.
6. Dip dough balls into egg whites, and then roll in ground walnuts.
7. Place on cookie sheet and bake just for 5 minutes.
8. Remove from oven; make thumbprint in center of each cookie, then fill with small amount of blueberry jam.
9. Return to oven and bake 10 minutes longer.
10. Allow to cool before removing from cookie sheet.

Yields: 4½ dozen.

Blueberry Walnut Bars

These bars make a great-tasting after-school snack which keeps very well.

Ingredients:

- 1   c. sugar
- 1   c. butter, room temperature
- 1   egg
- ½   tsp. almond extract
- 2¼ c. all-purpose flour
- 1   c. chopped walnuts
  blueberry sauce (recipe page 186)

Directions:

1. In large bowl cream sugar and butter; add egg and almond extract, mixing well.
2. Combine flour and walnuts; add to creamed mixture and blend well.
3. Reserve ⅓ of mixture; press remaining ⅔ onto bottom of greased 9 x 9-inch baking pan; refrigerate for at least 1 hour.
4. Preheat oven to 350 degrees F.
5. Remove from refrigerator, and spread blueberry sauce over cold dough in pan.
6. Sprinkle reserved crumb mixture over top, and bake for about 45 minutes.
7. Remove from oven, and cool completely before cutting into bars or squares.

Yields: 20 servings.

Blueberry Almond Cookies

This blue cookie is full of blueberries and almonds.

Ingredients:

1   pt. fresh blueberries
1½ c. sugar
1   c. butter, softened
2   eggs
1½ c. all-purpose flour
1½ c. whole-wheat flour
1½ tsp. baking soda
1   tsp. salt
1   c. chopped almonds

Directions:

1. Preheat oven to 350 degrees F.
2. Line baking sheets with aluminum foil or parchment paper.
3. Purée blueberries in food processor or blender.
4. In medium bowl cream sugar and butter together.
5. Beat in eggs, and then stir in blueberry purée.
6. Sift together flours, baking soda, and salt; stir into blueberry mixture.
7. Stir in chopped almonds.
8. Drop dough by heaping teaspoonfuls onto prepared cookie sheets.
9. Bake for 13 to 15 minutes.
10. Remove to wire racks to cool.

Yields: 2 dozen.

Did You Know? . . . .

Did you know that wild blueberries, smaller than cultivated ones, are prized for their intense color?

Blueberry Cookies

These blueberry cookies are simple to make and quite tasty.

Ingredients:

2½ c. all-purpose flour
2 tsp. baking powder
1 pinch salt
½ c. butter, softened
1 c. sugar
2 eggs, beaten
½ tsp. lemon extract
½ c. milk
1 c. fresh blueberries

Directions:

1. Preheat oven to 375 degrees F.
2. Grease cookie sheets.
3. Sift together flour, baking powder, and salt.
4. In large bowl cream butter and sugar.
5. Beat in eggs and lemon extract.
6. Mix in milk and flour mixture alternately in three parts, starting with milk.
7. Gently mix in blueberries.
8. Drop batter by tablespoonfuls onto prepared sheets, 1½ inches apart.
9. Bake 12 to 15 minutes.
10. Remove to wire rack to cool.

Yields: 2 dozen.

Did You Know? . . . .

Did you know that Southern Highbush berries are now also cultivated in the Mediterranean regions of Europe?

Oatmeal Blueberry Cookies

Oatmeal cookies are always a favorite. Raisins, dried cranberries, or dates can be substituted for the dried blueberries in this recipe.

Ingredients:

    1 c. whole-wheat flour
    1 tsp. baking soda
    1 tsp. salt
    1 tsp. ground cinnamon
    1 c. butter, softened
    ¾ c. brown sugar, firmly packed
    ¾ c. sugar
    2 eggs
    1 tsp. vanilla extract
    2 c. oatmeal
    ¾ c. dried blueberries (recipe page 253)

Directions:

1. Preheat oven to 350 degrees F.
2. Mix together flour, soda, salt, and cinnamon in small bowl.
3. Cream together butter and sugars in large bowl.
4. Mix in eggs and vanilla, and then stir in flour mixture.
5. Stir in oats and blueberries.
6. Drop by rounded tablespoonfuls onto cookie sheet sprayed with cooking spray.
7. Bake for 12 to 15 minutes, depending how soft you like your cookies.
8. Remove cookies to wire rack to cool.

Yields: 3 dozen.

Wild Blueberry Cookies

Wild blueberries, with their stronger flavor, are a great addition to these cookies.

Ingredients:

1¾ c. all-purpose flour
2 tsp. baking powder
½ tsp. salt
¾ c. wild blueberries, fresh or frozen, unthawed
½ c. butter, softened
1 c. sugar
1½ tsp. grated lemon rind
1 egg
¼ c. milk

Directions:

1. Preheat oven to 375 degrees F.
2. In large bowl combine flour, baking powder, and salt.
3. Stir in blueberries. (Frozen blueberries may be folded in quickly at the end since the dough turns purple as they thaw.)
4. Cream butter until soft; gradually beat in sugar, then lemon rind and egg.
5. Add flour mixture alternately with milk, beating until smooth after each addition.
6. Drop by teaspoonfuls onto greased cookie sheet.
7. Bake for 10 to 12 minutes or until lightly browned.
8. Transfer to wire rack to cool.

Yields: 3 dozen.

Blueberry and Lemon Crumb Bars

These bars are rich and delicious.

Ingredients for crust:

    1½ c. all-purpose flour
    2   Tbs. sugar
    2   tsp. grated lemon rind
    ¼   tsp. salt
    ½   c. unsalted cold butter, cut in ¼-inch slices
    1   lg. egg yolk
    1   tsp. vanilla extract
    1   Tbs. cold water (optional)

Ingredients for filling:

    ½   c. sugar
    2   Tbs. all-purpose flour
    ¼   tsp. freshly ground nutmeg
    2   c. blueberries, rinsed, sorted

Ingredients for topping:

    5   Tbs. unsalted butter, softened
    ½   c. light brown sugar, firmly packed
    ¾   c. all-purpose flour
        confectioners' sugar

Directions for crust:

1. Preheat oven to 400 degrees F.
2. Lightly butter 13 x 9 x 2-inch baking pan.
3. Combine flour, sugar, lemon zest, and salt in bowl of food processor.
4. With motor running add pats of cold butter a few at a time.

5. In small cup stir together egg yolk and vanilla.
6. With motor running, gradually add yolk mixture; process until mixture pulls together.
7. If mixture seems dry, add some to all of the cold water.
8. Turn dough out (it will be crumbly) into prepared pan.
9. With floured fingertips carefully press dough into even layer over bottom of pan.

Directions for filling:

1. In large bowl stir together sugar, flour, and nutmeg until blended.
2. Add blueberries; stir to coat.
3. Spread blueberry-sugar mixture in even layer over crust.

Directions for topping:

1. Work butter and sugar together with wooden spoon until blended.
2. Using fork, gradually add flour, stirring until mixture resembles coarse crumbs.
3. Sprinkle mixture evenly over blueberries.
4. Bake for 15 minutes; reduce oven temperature to 350 degrees F., and bake for 25 to 30 minutes longer or until edges and topping are browned and blueberries are cooked.
5. Cool on wire rack before cutting into bars.
6. Lightly sprinkle with confectioners' sugar before serving.

Yields: 24 to 30 servings.

Blueberry Drops

These make a great-tasting drop cookie that can be left underbaked for a softer cookie, or leave it in the oven longer for a crisper cookie.

Ingredients:

- ½ c. butter, softened
- 1 c. sugar
- ¾ c. brown sugar, firmly packed
- 1 egg, lightly beaten
- ¼ c. milk
- 2 Tbs. orange juice concentrate, thawed
- 3 c. all-purpose flour
- 1 tsp. baking powder
- ½ tsp. baking soda
- 1 c. chopped or ground walnuts
- 2½ c. frozen blueberries, thawed, rinsed, patted dry

Directions:

1. Cream butter and sugars.
2. Add egg, milk, and orange juice concentrate.
3. Sift together flour, baking powder, and baking soda.
4. Combine with creamed mixture, then add nuts and blueberries.
5. Drop dough by teaspoonfuls onto greased baking sheet; bake 10 to 12 minutes.
6. Transfer to wire rack to cool.

Yields: 10 dozen.

Blueberry Delights Cookbook

A Collection of Blueberry Recipes
Cookbook Delights Series-Book 2

Desserts

Table of Contents

Page

Blueberry Buckle

This standard buckle recipe is easy to make.

Ingredients for buckle:

> 2 c. all-purpose flour
> 2 tsp. baking powder
> ¼ c. butter, softened
> 1 c. sugar
> 1 egg
> ½ c. milk
> 2 c. blueberries

Ingredients for streusel topping:

> ½ c. sugar
> ½ c. all-purpose flour
> 1 tsp. ground cinnamon
> ½ c. chopped walnuts
> ¼ c. butter

Directions for buckle:

1. Preheat oven to 375 degrees F.
2. Sift together flour and baking powder.
3. In medium bowl cream butter, sugar, and egg.
4. Combine with mixed dry ingredients and milk.
5. Pour into greased and floured 9 x 9-inch baking pan.

Directions for streusel topping:

1. Mix sugar, flour, cinnamon, and walnuts.
2. Cut in butter, then sprinkle over blueberries.
3. Bake for about 45 minutes.

Yields: 4 to 6 servings.

Blueberry Crisp with Cinnamon Streusel Topping

A crisp is best served hot out of the oven topped with whipped cream. The crunchy streusel on this crisp is quite delicious.

Ingredients:

- 8 c. fresh blueberries (seven 6-oz. baskets), divided
- ¾ c. plus 6 Tbs. sugar, divided
- 1¾ c. all-purpose flour
- 1 c. finely chopped walnuts
- 6 Tbs. dark brown sugar, firmly packed
- 1 tsp. ground cinnamon
- ½ tsp. salt
- ¾ c. unsalted butter, melted, cooled
  Sweetened Whipped Cream (recipe page 238)

Directions:

1. Preheat oven to 350 degrees F.
2. Combine 2½ cups blueberries and ¾ cup sugar in large saucepan.
3. Cook over low heat until berries soften and release their juices, stirring frequently, about 8 minutes.
4. Mix in remaining blueberries.
5. Transfer mixture to 13 x 9 x 2-inch glass baking dish.
6. Mix flour, walnuts, brown sugar, cinnamon, salt, and remaining 6 tablespoons sugar in large bowl to blend.
7. Gradually add cooled, melted butter, mixing with fork until small moist clumps form.
8. Sprinkle streusel over berries.
9. Bake until topping is crisp and golden and filling is bubbling, about 45 minutes.
10. Cool slightly, then serve with whipped cream.

Yields: 8 to 10 servings.

Blueberry Nectarine Buckle

The combination of blueberries and nectarines is very tasty. You may substitute peaches for the nectarines if you desire.

Ingredients for topping:

- ¼ c. cold unsalted butter, cut into bits
- ½ c. sugar
- ⅓ c. all-purpose flour
- ½ tsp. ground cinnamon
- ½ tsp. freshly grated nutmeg

Ingredients for batter:

- ¾ c. unsalted butter, softened
- ¾ c. sugar
- 1 tsp. vanilla extract
- 1⅓ c. all-purpose flour
- ¼ tsp. baking powder
- ½ tsp. salt
- 3 lg. eggs
- 2 c. blueberries, picked over, rinsed
- 2 nectarines, pitted, cut into 1-inch wedges
  Sweetened Whipped Cream (recipe page 238) or ice cream

Directions for topping:

1. In small bowl blend together butter, sugar, flour, cinnamon, and nutmeg until mixture resembles coarse meal.
2. Chill while making batter.

Directions for batter:

1. Preheat oven to 350 degrees F.
2. In small bowl using electric mixer, cream together butter and sugar; beat in vanilla.

3. In another small bowl stir together flour, baking powder, and salt.
4. Beat flour mixture into butter mixture alternately with eggs, adding one egg at a time, beating well after each addition.
5. Fold in blueberries and nectarines.
6. Spread batter in well-buttered 10 x 2-inch round cake pan or 2-quart baking pan.
7. Sprinkle topping evenly over top.
8. Bake for 45 to 50 minutes or until tester comes out clean and topping is crisp and golden.
9. Serve with whipped cream or ice cream.

Blueberry Sorbet

Sorbet makes a great-tasting, light finish to a meal.

Ingredients:

8 c. fresh blueberries, lightly rinsed, dried
¾ c. sugar
¼ c. fresh lemon juice
½ c. water
   blueberries for garnish (optional)
   fresh mint for garnish (optional)

Directions:

1. Purée blueberries in blender.
2. Transfer to medium pot.
3. Add sugar, lemon juice, and water.
4. Bring to a boil then remove from heat.
5. Strain into bowl and set aside to cool.
6. When cool, freeze in ice cream maker according to manufacturer's instructions.
7. Garnish with blueberries and fresh mint if desired.
8. Note: Once sorbet softens, it does not refreeze well.

Yields: 6 servings (½ cup each).

Blueberry Steamed Pudding

This version of steamed pudding is absolutely wonderful.

Ingredients:

- 5 Tbs. butter, divided
- ¾ c. plus 1 Tbs. sugar, divided
- 4 c. blueberries, fresh or frozen, unthawed, divided
- ½ c. all-purpose flour
- ½ c. vanilla yogurt
- 1 tsp. vanilla extract
- 6 eggs

Directions:

1. Using 1 tablespoon butter, grease 1½-quart microwave-safe round baking dish or bowl, and sprinkle with 1 tablespoon sugar; set aside.
2. In large microwave-safe dish, toss 2 cups blueberries and remaining ¾ cup sugar.
3. Cover loosely with clear plastic wrap, and microwave on high (100% power) until blueberries are tender, about 4 minutes.
4. In container of food processor, combine cooked blueberries, flour, yogurt, vanilla, and remaining 4 tablespoons butter; process until smooth.
5. Add eggs; pulse to blend.
6. Pour mixture into prepared dish, and then stir in remaining 2 cups blueberries.
7. Cover dish loosely with plastic wrap, and microwave on high until set in center, 12 to 14 minutes.
8. Prick plastic wrap to release steam; cover dish with large plate, and let stand 20 to 30 minutes.
9. Uncover and remove plastic wrap; invert pudding onto serving plate.

10. Serve warm with additional vanilla yogurt if desired.
11. Note: This recipe was tested in a 625-watt microwave oven.

Yields: 8 servings.

Minted Blueberries with Lemon Cream

This refreshing dessert can be prepared in 45 minutes or less. Serve it with a fancy cookie on the side.

Ingredients:

    2   Tbs. water
    2   Tbs. sugar, divided
    ½   pt. picked-over blueberries
    1½ tsp. chopped fresh mint leaves
    ½   c. heavy cream, well chilled
    1   tsp. finely grated fresh lemon zest

Directions:

1. In very small saucepan simmer water and 1 tablespoon sugar until sugar is dissolved, about 1 minute.
2. In small bowl toss syrup with blueberries and mint.
3. Chill blueberry mixture, covered, 15 minutes or until cold.
4. Divide blueberries between 2 martini glasses.
5. In chilled bowl with electric mixer, beat cream with remaining tablespoon sugar until it just holds stiff peaks; fold in zest.
6. Top blueberries with lemon cream and serve.

Yields: 2 servings.

Flaming Blueberries Brandy

This is suitable to be prepared tableside in a chafing dish.

Ingredients:

¼ c. butter
½ c. brown sugar, firmly packed
4 Tbs. brandy or rum
1 can blueberries, drained
vanilla ice cream

Directions:

1. Melt butter in heavy skillet.
2. Add brown sugar, stirring until it melts.
3. Add berries, stirring gently until heated through, about 1 minute.
4. Sprinkle brandy over and ignite.
5. Pour berries and liquid mixture over individual servings of ice cream.

Yields: 6 servings.

Russian Cream with Blueberries

This dessert is easy to make. It can be made ahead and served with your favorite berries.

Ingredients:

3 c. sugar
4 env. unflavored gelatin
2 c. cold water
1 qt. heavy cream
6 c. sour cream
1 Tbs. plus 1 tsp. vanilla extract
blueberries

Directions:

1. Mix sugar and gelatin in saucepan.
2. Add water and mix well.
3. Allow to stand approximately 5 minutes.
4. Bring to full boil, stirring constantly.
5. Remove from heat; add heavy cream to mixture.
6. In stainless steel bowl whisk together sour cream and vanilla.
7. Gradually whisk sugar-gelatin mixture into sour cream mixture until smooth.
8. Pour into bowl; cover with plastic wrap and chill until set, at least 4 hours.
9. Serve with fresh blueberries and a crisp cookie.

Blueberry Raspberry Sorbet

Blueberries and raspberries blend to make a great- tasting sorbet.

Ingredients:

10 oz. blueberries
10 oz. raspberries
1½ c. sugar
   juice of 2 oranges
   juice of 1 lemon

Directions:

1. Rinse and drain berries.
2. In food processor purée berries with orange and lemon juices and sugar.
3. Strain purée and discard any seeds.
4. Pour preparation into ice cream machine, and churn sorbet.
5. When ready, transfer to pre-chilled mold or bowl covered with lid or plastic film, place in freezer, and use within 3 days.

Blueberry Ice Cream

Our family loves ice cream, and the addition of blueberries makes this a very tasty treat. This ice cream is made without using an ice cream maker.

Ingredients:

- 1 pkg. unflavored gelatin
- ½ c. cold milk
- ½ c. milk, heated to boiling
- 2 c. blueberries, fresh or dry-pack frozen, thawed
- ¾ c. sugar
- 2 c. whipping cream, whipped

Directions:

1. In 5-cup blender, sprinkle unflavored gelatin over cold milk; let stand 3 to 4 minutes.
2. Add hot milk and process at low speed until gelatin is completely dissolved, about 2 minutes.
3. Let cool completely.
4. Add blueberries and sugar; process at high speed until blended.
5. Pour into large bowl and chill, stirring occasionally, until mixture mounds slightly when dropped from a spoon.
6. Fold whipped cream into gelatin mixture.
7. Pour into two 4 x 10-inch freezer trays or one 8-inch baking pan; freeze until firm.

Yields: 1½ quarts.

Did You Know? . . . .

Did you know that by the early 1980s, the blueberry industry was started in New Zealand and is still growing?

Blueberry Maple Cobbler

The added flavor of maple makes this cobbler a great brunch dessert. It is delicious served warm with ice cream.

Ingredients:

2½ c. blueberries
⅔ c. maple-flavored syrup
½ c. all-purpose flour
1 tsp. baking powder
1 pinch salt
½ tsp. ground cinnamon
1 Tbs. freshly grated orange rind
2 Tbs. butter, melted
1 Tbs. milk

Directions:

1. Preheat oven to 400 degrees F.
2. Cook blueberries and maple syrup in saucepan over moderate heat, stirring occasionally until berries are soft.
3. Remove from heat.
4. Sift together flour, baking powder, salt, and cinnamon.
5. Combine with orange rind, melted butter, and milk.
6. Turn dough out on lightly floured surface, and roll out with floured rolling pin to make 9-inch disk about ⅛ inch thick.
7. Transfer berry mixture into 9-inch pie dish, place dough crust on top, and bake for 25 minutes.
8. Allow to cool a little before serving.
9. Serve with ice cream.

Yields: 6 servings.

Blueberry Shortcake

Most of us are used to strawberry shortcake, but blueberry makes a flavorful and colorful change.

Ingredients for biscuits:

1¾ c. all-purpose flour
3 Tbs. baking powder
¼ tsp. salt
½ c. sugar
4 Tbs. butter
¾ c. milk

Ingredients for topping:

2 c. fresh blueberries
¾ c. sugar
6 scoops vanilla ice cream
additional blueberries
Sweetened Whipped Cream (recipe page 238)

Directions for biscuits:

1. Preheat oven to 425 degrees F.
2. Combine flour, baking powder, salt, and sugar in medium mixing bowl; cut in butter with pastry knife until mixture resembles small peas.
3. Quickly stir in milk, and mix with wooden spoon for 30 seconds.
4. Spread onto well-floured surface, and knead gently for 15 seconds.
5. Roll to ½-inch thickness, and cut into 3-inch circles with round cookie cutter or jar cap; place on baking sheet.
6. Bake for 12 to 20 minutes or until golden.

Directions for topping and assembly:

1. Combine blueberries and sugar in blender; blend until thick purée forms.
2. On 6 individual plates pour 3 tablespoons blueberry purée.
3. On top of purée, place bottom half of biscuits that have been sliced in half horizontally.
4. Place whole fresh blueberries and whipped cream on top of each biscuit; add scoop of ice cream.
5. Top with other half of biscuit, and garnish over all with more purée, blueberries, and whipped cream in an attractive manner.
6. Serve immediately.

Yields: 6 servings.

Blueberry Flummery

Try this blueberry flummery for a different dessert dish after your favorite dinner.

Ingredients:

2 Tbs. cornstarch
½ c. sugar
1½ c. water
2 c. blueberries, fresh or dry-pack frozen, rinsed, drained
    juice and grated rind of 1 lemon
    twist of lemon peel
    thick cream

Directions:

1. Combine cornstarch and sugar.
2. Stir in water, blueberries, and lemon rind and juice.
3. Cook over low heat while stirring until flummery bubbles and thickens.
4. Spoon into sherbet glasses and chill.
5. Garnish with a twist of lemon peel.
6. Serve with thick cream.

Blueberry Heaven Cheesecake

This is an easy-to-make, tasty cheesecake.

Ingredients for crust:

- 1   c. all-purpose flour
- ¼   lb. butter, softened
- 2   Tbs. confectioners' sugar

Ingredients for filling:

- 2   pkg. cream cheese (3 oz. each), softened
- 1   tsp. vanilla extract
- ½   c. confectioners' sugar
- 1   c. whipping cream

Ingredients for topping:

- 1   c. sugar
- 2¼ c. fresh berries, divided
- 3   Tbs. cornstarch

Directions for crust:

1. Preheat oven to 425 degrees F.
2. Mix together flour, butter, and confectioners' sugar; pat into buttered pie plate.
3. Bake for 8 to 10 minutes; remove from oven and cool.

Directions for filling:

1. Beat cream cheese, vanilla, and confectioners' sugar, then fold in cream; pour into crust.
2. Chill 1 hour.

Directions for topping:

1. In saucepan cook and stir all ingredients until clear and thick.
2. Cool, then spread over top of filling.
3. Refrigerate until ready to serve.

Yields: 8 to 10 servings.

Blueberry Peach Whole-Wheat Crisp

This crisp adds a touch of whole-wheat for that whole-grain flavor. It is at its best served warm and topped with sweetened whipped cream or ice cream.

Ingredients:

    6-8 large peaches
    3   c. blueberries
    1½ c. sugar, divided
    ¼ c. whole-wheat flour
    1   tsp. baking powder
    ¼ tsp. salt
    ½ tsp. ground cinnamon
    1   Tbs. butter
    1   egg, beaten
    Sweetened Whipped Cream (recipe page 238) or ice cream

Directions:

1. Preheat oven to 375 degrees F.
2. Peel and halve peaches.
3. Remove pits and slice each fruit into 6 pieces.
4. Place in greased 13 x 9 x 2-inch baking pan.
5. Arrange blueberries over peaches, and sprinkle with 1 cup sugar.
6. Mix flour, baking powder, remaining ½ cup sugar, salt, and cinnamon.
7. Combine with butter and egg in food processor or by hand.
8. Crumble over fruit.
9. Bake for about 45 minutes.
10. Serve warm with whipped cream or ice cream.

Yields: 8 generous servings.

Blueberry Slump

Slump is an interesting name for a dessert, but this recipe is quite tasty.

Ingredients:

    4   c. blueberries, fresh or frozen, rinsed, drained
    1¾ c. sugar, divided
    3   Tbs. butter, softened
    ½   c. milk
    1   c. all-purpose flour
    1   tsp. baking powder
    ½   tsp. salt, divided
    1½ Tbs. cornstarch
    1   c. boiling water

Directions:

1. Preheat oven to 375 degrees F.
2. Place blueberries in 13 x 9 x 2-inch baking pan.
3. Mix ¾ cup sugar, butter, milk, flour, baking powder, and ¼ teaspoon salt to batter consistency.
4. Pour over fruit.
5. Mix remaining ¼ teaspoon salt, remaining 1 cup sugar, and cornstarch.
6. Sprinkle over top of batter.
7. Pour boiling water over all.
8. Bake 1 hour (longer if berries are frozen); batter will be browned on top when done.

Did You Know? . . . .

Did you know that in the Southern hemisphere, Chile, Argentina, New Zealand, and Australia now export blueberries?

Blueberry Timbales

These attractive timbales make a nice dessert presentation and are great served with vanilla ice cream. Green honeydew makes an attractive color contrast with the blue-purple blueberries.

Ingredients:

¼ c. cold water
2 env. unflavored gelatin
2 c. blueberries
1 c. sugar
½ tsp. almond extract
2 c. plain yogurt
raspberry sherbet
honeydew melon chunks
Sweetened Whipped Cream (recipe page 238)

Directions:

1. Sprinkle gelatin over cold water, and let stand.
2. Purée blueberries in blender and pour into saucepan.
3. Stir in sugar and softened gelatin.
4. Cook over moderate heat, stirring until mixture boils.
5. Remove from heat and stir in almond extract; cool.
6. When cooled to room temperature, whisk in yogurt; spoon into fluted timbale molds sprayed with nonstick cooking spray.
7. Refrigerate at least 4 hours.
8. Turn timbales onto individual dessert plates, and arrange with raspberry sherbet and honeydew chunks.
9. Garnish with whipped cream.

Fresh Blueberry Custard Parfait

Custard and berries go very well together, making this a very flavorful and attractive dessert.

Ingredients:

¼ c. plus 1 Tbs. sugar, divided
¼ tsp. salt
2 lg. eggs, slightly beaten
1½ c. milk
1 tsp. vanilla extract
1 tsp. grated orange peel
½ tsp. grated lemon peel
¼ tsp. ground nutmeg
⅓ c. whipping cream
2 c. fresh blueberries

Directions:

1. Combine ¼ cup sugar and salt in top of double boiler.
2. Blend in eggs and milk.
3. Stir and cook over hot water (not boiling) until custard coats wooden spoon.
4. Remove from heat; cool.
5. Stir in vanilla, orange and lemon peel, and nutmeg.
6. Whip cream with remaining 1 tablespoon sugar until cream holds its shape; fold into custard mixture.
7. Arrange alternate layers of blueberries and custard in parfait glasses; chill.

Did You Know? . . . .

Did you know that the town of Oxford, Nova Scotia, is known as the Wild Blueberry Capital of Canada?

Blueberry Nectarine Crisp

My family enjoys baked fruit crisps. This is a nice variation and is also great served warm with vanilla ice cream.

Ingredients:

  6 med. nectarines
  2 c. blueberries
  ¾ c. plus 4 Tbs. sugar, divided
  1 c. all-purpose flour
  1 tsp. salt
  2 tsp. baking powder
  1 egg beaten
  ¼ c. butter, melted
  1 tsp. ground cinnamon
  Sweetened Whipped Cream (recipe page 238)

Directions:

  1. Preheat oven to 375 degrees F.
  2. Halve, pit, and cut nectarines into wedges (6 from each fruit).
  3. Butter 8 x 12-inch baking dish, and place nectarine wedges on bottom.
  4. Arrange blueberries over top of nectarines.
  5. Sprinkle with 3 tablespoons sugar.
  6. Mix flour, ¾ cup sugar, salt, and baking powder.
  7. Add beaten egg and melted butter; mix with fork, then by hand.
  8. Crumble on top fruit.
  9. Combine remaining 1 tablespoon sugar with cinnamon, and sprinkle on top.
  10. Bake for 30 minutes.
  11. Serve warm with whipped cream or ice cream.

Yields: 6 to 8 servings.

Raspberry Blueberry Cobbler

Blueberries and raspberries go great together, and this easy-to-make cobbler is a nice ending to any meal.

Ingredients:

- 1   c. blueberries
- 1   c. raspberries
- 1   c. sugar, divided
- ½   c. water
- ¼   c. butter, softened
- 1   c. all-purpose flour
- 1½ tsp. baking powder
- ¼   tsp. salt
- 1   egg, slightly beaten
- ½   c. milk
- 1   tsp. vanilla extract
- Sweetened Whipped Cream (recipe page 238)

Directions:

1. Preheat oven to 375 degrees F.
2. Mix berries, ½ cup sugar, and water in saucepan.
3. Cook over moderate heat until berries are soft.
4. Pour into a 9 x 9-inch baking dish.
5. Cream butter and remaining ½ cup sugar.
6. Sift together flour, baking powder, and salt.
7. Add to creamed mixture along with egg, milk, and vanilla, beating well.
8. Spoon over berries, and bake for about 30 minutes.
9. Serve warm with whipped cream or vanilla ice cream.

Yields: 6 servings.

Blueberry Delights Cookbook
A Collection of Blueberry Recipes
Cookbook Delights Series-Book 2

Dressings, Sauces, and Condiments

Table of Contents

Did You Know?....

Did you know that true wild blueberries occur only in eastern North America?

Blueberry Barbeque Sauce

This makes a flavorful blueberry barbeque sauce. With it, you can add the great taste of blueberry to roasted or grilled turkey, chicken, or pork.

Ingredients:

- 2 qt. blueberries, fresh or frozen
- 1½ c. celery
- 1½ c. finely chopped onion
- 1½ c. finely chopped red pepper
- 1 garlic clove, minced well
- 1 carrot, shredded fine
- ½ c. honey or to taste
- 2 Tbs. molasses
- 1 c. vinegar
- 1½ tsp. salt
- 1½ tsp. pepper
- 1 Tbs. paprika
- 1 tsp. ground cinnamon
- ⅛ tsp. ground nutmeg or to taste
- ⅓ tsp. dry mustard or to taste
- ⅛ tsp. ground cloves or to taste
- ⅛ tsp. celery seed or as desired
- ⅛ tsp. ground ginger or to taste
  cayenne pepper to taste

Directions:

1. Thaw blueberries if frozen, but do not drain; purée.
2. Combine celery, onion, red pepper, garlic, and carrot in large saucepan; add honey, molasses, and vinegar, stirring well.
3. Add salt and pepper; blend in spices.
4. Add puréed berries and mix well.
5. Simmer over medium heat, stirring occasionally, until thickened.

Yields: 4 cups.

Blueberry Caramel Sauce

This sauce is great served over your favorite ice cream or pound cake.

Ingredients:

- ½ c. sugar
- ¼ c. water
- 2 Tbs. orange juice
- 1 c. heavy or whipping cream
- ½ tsp. vanilla extract
- 1 pt. fresh blueberries
- fresh blueberries for garnish

Directions:

1. Bring sugar and water to boil in medium saucepan over medium-high heat.
2. Reduce heat to medium; cook, swirling pan occasionally, until mixture is caramel colored, 5 to 10 minutes.
3. Remove from heat, and carefully stir in orange juice with long-handled wooden spoon, stirring vigorously until blended. (Use caution as mixture will bubble.)
4. Return pan to heat; stir in heavy cream.
5. Bring to boil; reduce heat and simmer sauce until thickened and reduced to 1 cup, about 8 minutes.
6. Stir in vanilla; pour sauce into medium bowl, and stir in blueberries.
7. If not using immediately, cover and refrigerate for up to 4 days.

Yields: 8 servings.

Did You Know? . . . .

Did you know that South Africa exports blueberries to Europe?

Blueberry Grape Dressing

This mixture of flavors makes a very tasty dressing for use on baby greens or lightly wilted spinach.

Ingredients:

- 3 Tbs. honey
- 1 c. grape juice
- 1 c. fresh blueberries
- 2 Tbs. shallots, minced
- 1 c. extra-virgin olive oil
  sea salt to taste
  freshly ground black pepper to taste

Directions:

1. Warm honey slightly, and then place in food processor with grape juice, blueberries, and shallots.
2. Drizzle olive oil into mixture slowly while machine is blending. (Emulsification is not critical.)
3. For wilted spinach salad, take 1 ounce of dressing per person and a handful of spinach leaves; wilt lightly in pan.
4. We often add bits of cooked applewood smoked bacon, roasted bell peppers, toasted pine nuts, and dollops of fromage blanc around the outside.

Berry Butter

This is a versatile recipe. You can substitute strawberries or raspberries for the blueberries. Spread it on pancakes, waffles, muffins, or bagels for a tasty treat.

Ingredients:

- 1 c. fresh blueberries
- 1 c. butter, softened
- 3 Tbs. light corn syrup

Directions:

1. In 5-cup blender container or food processor, purée berries.
2. If necessary press through sieve to remove seeds or skins; set aside.
3. In small mixer bowl, beat butter until light and fluffy, 1 to 2 minutes.
4. Add berry purée and corn syrup to butter; beat at medium speed until well mixed.
5. Cover and refrigerate.
6. Let stand at room temperature 30 minutes before serving.

Yields: 2 cups.

Blueberry Basil Vinegar

This is a flavorful blend of blueberry and basil. It makes a great gift when packaged in a decorative jar.

Ingredients:

    3 c. fresh blueberries, crushed
    ½ c. firmly packed, torn fresh basil leaves
    4 c. white vinegar
       fresh basil leaves (optional)

Directions:

1. Combine blueberries and basil in large, sterilized wide-mouth jar, and set aside.
2. Place vinegar in medium nonreactive saucepan, and bring to a boil.
3. Pour hot vinegar over blueberry mixture; cover jar, and let stand at room temperature for 2 weeks.

Yields: 4 cups.

Blueberry Ketchup

The potpourri of spices in this ketchup makes it very flavorful.

Ingredients:

    2 Tbs. vegetable oil
    1 lg. garlic clove, crushed
    1 Tbs. minced fresh ginger
    1 med. onion, finely chopped
    2 pt. blueberries
    1 c. fresh tomato, peeled, seeded, chopped
    2 lg. purple plums, pitted, chopped
    ¼ c. dark brown sugar, firmly packed
    1 Tbs. blueberry vinegar (recipe page 188)
    1 Tbs. fresh lemon juice
    1 med. dried chili pepper, crumbled
    1 tsp. ground cinnamon
    1 tsp. ground cardamom
    1 tsp. ground coriander
    1 tsp. salt
    1 tsp. freshly ground mixed peppercorns
    zest of 1 lemon, cut into julienne strips

Directions:

1. Heat oil in 2-quart or larger, heavy-bottom saucepan; add garlic and ginger, and cook over low heat for 2 minutes.
2. Add onion; cook until soft and transparent, stirring often.
3. Add blueberries, tomato, plums, brown sugar, vinegar, lemon juice and zest, chili pepper, spices, salt, and pepper, stirring well.
4. Cook over medium heat until mixture begins to simmer.

5. Reduce heat and simmer gently for 30 minutes.
6. Remove from heat and let mixture cool slightly.
7. Purée in food processor or blender.
8. Return purée to pan and heat, bringing mixture to a simmer; cook until thick, about 1 hour.
9. Pour into 2 sterile pint jars or containers.
10. Cover and cool.
11. Store in refrigerator for up to 4 weeks or freeze.

Yields: 2 pints.

Blueberry Relish

This relish goes great with your favorite hamburger, hot dog, or polish sausage. Make sure everything is coarsely chopped.

Ingredients:
- ¼ c. Vidalia onion, diced
- ¼ c. balsamic vinegar
- 2 Tbs. sugar
- 1 Tbs. fresh lemon juice
- 1½ c. blueberries, washed
  salt and pepper to taste

Directions:
1. If using food processor, coarsely chop 1 small onion wedge and measure ¼ cup.
2. Return to processor and add remaining ingredients, or dice onion and berries by hand and mix with remaining ingredients.
3. Let sit at room temperature for 20 minutes or until meal is served.

Yields: 1½ cups.

Blueberry Orange Vinegar

This flavorful vinegar makes a nice gift.

Ingredients:

- 2 pt. blueberries, washed, drained
- 1 c. sugar
  vinegar to cover
  zest of 1 orange

Directions:

1. Place blueberries in large bowl.
2. Cover with vinegar and let stand for 1 hour.
3. Transfer to large nonreactive saucepan.
4. Add sugar and orange zest; bring to a boil.
5. Reduce heat, cover, and simmer for 20 minutes.
6. Strain through fine sieve or double layer of cheesecloth, pressing out as much liquid as possible.
7. Discard residue and pour liquid back into pan.
8. Heat through and pour into hot glass jars or fancy bottles.
9. Refrigerate after opening.

Blueberry Glaze

This is an ideal glaze to use with smoked meat, duck and pork, any game, chicken, or game hen.

Ingredients:

- 1 Tbs. butter
- 2 Tbs. minced shallots
- ½ oz. brandy
- 2 oz. crème de cassis liqueur
- 1 tsp. blueberry jelly (recipe page 205) or 1 tsp. sugar and ½ c. blueberries
- ½ c. veal stock or beef broth
- ¼ c. whole milk
  salt and pepper (optional)

Directions:

1. In large sauté pan melt butter over medium-high heat; add shallots and cook until light brown.
2. Add brandy, crème de cassis liqueur, and jelly or blueberry mix; reduce until almost dry.
3. Add veal or beef broth, and heat until reduced by half.
4. Remove from heat and swirl in milk; season to taste with salt and pepper if desired.
5. To serve, slice and arrange cooked meat on warm plate or platter, pour hot glaze over meat, and serve immediately.

Blueberry Salsa

Serve this unique salsa as a condiment or topping with any foods desired.

Ingredients:

1 pt. blueberries
1 pt. strawberries
¼ c. sugar
3 Tbs. minced sweet onion
1 Tbs. raspberry vinegar or lemon juice
1 tsp. freshly ground black pepper
¼ c. sliced or slivered almonds, toasted
    hot pepper sauce to taste

Directions:

1. Rinse blueberries and strawberries; dry on paper towels.
2. Sort over berries; hull strawberries and cut into quarters.
3. In bowl combine all ingredients except almonds.
4. Mix well and refrigerate for at least 1 hour.
5. Just before serving, stir in almonds.

Yields: 3½ cups.

Fresh Blueberry Sauce

This is a thick and flavorful blueberry sauce. Spoon it warm over your favorite food. You can also serve this sauce as a dessert. Just cool it in the refrigerator, spoon into bowls, and top with sweetened whipped cream.

Ingredients:

½ c. sugar
1½ Tbs. cornstarch
2 c. blueberries
⅓ c. water
2 Tbs. lemon juice
dash ground nutmeg

Directions:

1. In saucepan combine sugar and cornstarch; stir in berries; add water and lemon juice.
2. Stir while cooking over medium heat until thickened.
3. Spoon over your favorite food while warm.
4. Sprinkle with dash of nutmeg, and add a fresh pansy or sprig of peppermint herb on plate as garnish.

Wild Blueberry Chutney

Try this spiced chutney with your poultry or main entrée for a wonderful taste variation.

Ingredients:

½ c. raspberry vinegar
½ c. sugar
1 med. onion, minced
¼ tsp. minced fresh ginger
⅛ tsp. ground cinnamon
1 tsp. minced lemon rind
1 pinch cayenne pepper
1 pinch salt
3 c. blueberries
¼ c. dried cranberries

Directions:

1. Combine vinegar, sugar, onion, ginger, cinnamon, lemon, pepper, and salt in saucepan; bring to a boil and simmer 15 minutes.
2. Add 1 cup blueberries and cranberries.
3. Simmer 20 minutes, stirring frequently.
4. Add remaining 2 cups blueberries, and simmer another 10 minutes.

Yields: Approximately 1 cup.

Wild Blueberry Vinaigrette

This vinaigrette is delicious on fresh spring mix greens.

Ingredients:

½ c. olive oil
¼ c. red wine or cider vinegar
2 Tbs. balsamic vinegar
1 clove garlic, minced
2 tsp. prepared mustard
½ tsp. salt
¼ tsp. pepper
½ c. wild blueberries, fresh or frozen, thawed

Directions:

1. Combine all ingredients except blueberries in jar and shake until thoroughly blended, or whisk thoroughly in bowl.
2. Add blueberries.
3. Store in refrigerator.

Yields: 1½ cups.

Blueberry Vinegar

This is very flavorful vinegar, so use it in place of the plainer varieties. It also makes an attractive gift when put in a decorative bottle.

Ingredients:

    1 c. blueberry juice (recipe page 252)
    ½ c. cider vinegar
    ¼ c. water
    2 Tbs. sugar

Directions:

1. In shaker jar combine juice, vinegar, water, and sugar; shake well.
2. Pour into sterilized bottle and refrigerate.
3. Keep refrigerated between uses.

Yields: About 1 pint.

Blueberry Dressing
(Low Fat)

Try serving this dressing over slices of watermelon and honeydew or in a cabbage slaw.

Ingredients:

    2 c. chopped or sliced mixed fresh berries (blueberries, raspberries, strawberries, or whatever is in season)
    2 Tbs. red wine vinegar
    2 tsp. dry red wine
    2 tsp. fresh orange juice
    ½ tsp. freshly ground black pepper

Directions:

1. In small nonreactive bowl combine all ingredients, and mix until well blended.
2. Cover and chill until ready to use.

Yields: 1½ cups.

Blueberry Apple Chutney

Serve this tasty chutney with turkey, roast game, or with rice and your favorite Indian food. Your family and guests will rave about this one, for sure!

Ingredients:

2 c. blueberries
6 green apples, cored, peeled, cubed
½ c. water
½ c. cider vinegar
1 lg. onion, chopped
1 c. sugar
1 tsp. salt
1 tsp. ground cinnamon
1 tsp. ground ginger
1 pinch ground cloves

Directions:

1. Combine blueberries, apples, water, vinegar, and onion in 4-quart cooking pot; stir well.
2. Heat completely then add sugar, salt, cinnamon, ginger, and cloves; cook over moderate heat about 1½ hours, adding more water if necessary.
3. If not serving immediately, cool, cover, and store in refrigerator for up to 3 days.
4. When ready to use, warm through and serve with turkey, roast game, or with rice and your favorite Indian food.

189

Blueberry Balsamic Vinegar

Our family loves balsamic vinegar. This flavorful blueberry version can be used in salad dressings or drizzled over grilled chicken or beef.

Ingredients:

    4 c. blueberries, fresh or frozen, thawed
    1 qt. balsamic vinegar
    ¼ c. sugar
    1 lime
    1 cinnamon stick

Directions:

1. In large nonreactive saucepan, crush blueberries with potato masher or back of heavy spoon.
2. Peel lime, cutting peel (green part only) into strips; squeeze juice.
3. Add vinegar, sugar, lime juice and peel, and cinnamon; bring to a boil.
4. Reduce heat and simmer, covered, for 20 minutes.
5. Cool slightly and pour into large bowl.
6. Cover; refrigerate for 2 days to allow flavors to blend.
7. Place wire-mesh strainer (or cheesecloth) over large bowl.
8. In batches, ladle blueberry mixture into strainer, pressing out as much liquid as possible; discard solids.
9. Pour vinegar into clean glass bottles or jars; refrigerate, tightly covered, indefinitely.

Yields: 5 cups.

Did You Know? . . . .

Did you know that blueberries were first introduced to Australia in the 1950s, but the effort was unsuccessful?

Blueberry Delights Cookbook

A Collection of Blueberry Recipes
Cookbook Delights Series-Book 2

Jams, Jellies, and Syrups

Table of Contents

Did You Know? . . . .

Did you know that blueberries grow in clusters on bushes?

A Basic Guide for Canning Jams, Jellies, and Syrups

1. Wash jars in hot, soapy water inside and out with brush or soft cloth.
2. Run your finger around rim of each jar, discarding any with cracks or chips.
3. Rinse well in clean, clear, hot water, using tongs to avoid burns to hands or fingers.
4. Place upside down on clean cloth to drain well.
5. Place lids in boiling water for 2 minutes to sterilize and keep hot until placing on rim of jar.
6. Immediately prior to filling each jar, immerse in very hot water with tongs to heat jar (avoids breakage of jar with hot liquid).
7. Fill jar to within 1 inch of top of rim or to level recommended in recipe.
8. Wipe rim with clean damp cloth to remove any particles of food, and check again for any chips or cracks.
9. With tongs, place lid from hot bath directly onto rim of jar.
10. Using gloves, cloth, or holders, tighten lid firmly onto jar with ring or use single formed lid in place of ring to cover inner lid. Do not tighten down too hard as it may impede sealing.
11. Place on protected surface to cool, taking care to not disturb lid and ring. A slight indentation of lid will be apparent when sealed.
12. Leave overnight until thoroughly cooled.
13. When cooled, wipe jars with damp cloth and then label and date each.
14. Store upright on shelf in cool dark place.

Blueberry Marmalade

This blueberry marmalade is delicious on toast, bagels, or English muffins.

Ingredients:

- 1 med. orange
- 1 med. lemon
- ¾ c. water
- ⅛ tsp. baking soda
- 4 c. fresh blueberries, crushed
- 5 c. sugar
- 1 pkg. liquid fruit pectin (6 oz.)

Directions:

1. Peel orange and lemon; finely chop rind and place in large cooking pan.
2. Chop orange and lemon pulp, and set aside.
3. Add water and baking soda to rind, and bring to a boil.
4. Reduce heat and simmer 10 minutes, stirring occasionally.
5. Add chopped orange and lemon pulp, blueberries, and sugar.
6. Return to a boil; reduce heat and simmer 5 minutes.
7. Remove from heat and cool 5 minutes.
8. Add pectin and return to a boil.
9. Boil, stirring constantly, for 1 minute.
10. Remove from heat, and skim off foam with metal spoon.
11. Pour into hot, sterilized jars, leaving ¼-inch headspace.
12. Wipe jar rims; cover at once with metal lids, and screw on bands.
13. Process in boiling water bath for 10 minutes, following canning directions on page 186.

Yields: 6 half pints.

Blueberry Jam

This is a simple recipe with the pure taste of blueberry.

Ingredients:

    6 c. blueberries
    1 lemon
    7 c. sugar
    1 bottle fruit pectin

Directions:

1. Rinse fruit thoroughly, and then crush.
2. Add lemon juice, grated rind of ½ lemon, and sugar; mix thoroughly.
3. Heat rapidly to full rolling boil, stirring constantly; boil hard 2 minutes.
4. Remove from heat and stir in fruit pectin.
5. Skim, then ladle into hot jars, and process in hot water bath, following canning directions on page 186.

Blueberry and Bing Cherry Jam

This makes a delicious jam combination of two favorites, blueberries and Bing cherries. This is great on your favorite toast, bagel, or English muffin.

Ingredients:

    3   c. blueberries
    2½ c. Bing cherries, pitted, chopped
    2   Tbs. lemon juice
    1   pkg. fruit pectin
    4   c. sugar
    1   tsp. almond extract

Directions:

1. Puree blueberries in blender.
2. In heavy pot combine blueberries with chopped Bing cherries, lemon juice, and pectin.
3. Bring to rolling boil over moderate heat, stirring constantly.
4. Add sugar all at once and bring mixture to boil again; continue stirring constantly.
5. Allow mixture to boil hard for 1 full minute.
6. Remove from heat, stir in almond extract, skim off foam, and ladle into sterilized hot jars.
7. Process following canning directions on page 186.

Yields: 6 to 7 half pints.

Blueberry Rhubarb Jam

This is a great way to use rhubarb. Combining it with blueberries makes a wonderfully tasty jam.

Ingredients:

1½ c. crushed blueberries
¾ c. cooked, mashed rhubarb
3½ c. sugar
1   pouch pectin (3 oz.)

Directions:

1. In large Dutch oven combine blueberries, rhubarb, and sugar; mix well.
2. Place over high heat and bring to a full boil.
3. Cook for 1 minute, stirring constantly.
4. Remove from heat and stir in pectin.
5. Alternately stir and skim for 5 minutes.
6. Discard floating fruit.
7. Ladle into hot, sterilized jars and seal, following canning directions on page 186.

Blueberry Preserves

This is a delicious blend of whole berry preserves with great texture and flavor.

Ingredients:

   6 c. blueberries
   1 Tbs. lemon juice
   1 pkg. fruit pectin
   4 c. sugar

Directions:

1. Rinse and drain blueberries.
2. Place in bowl and mash with potato masher. (This should yields 4 cups.)
3. In heavy pan, combine mashed blueberries with lemon juice and pectin.
4. Bring to rolling boil over medium-high heat, stirring constantly.
5. Add sugar all at once, stirring, and bring to boil again.
6. Allow to boil for 1 full minute.
7. Remove from heat, skim off foam, and ladle into sterilized, hot jars.
8. Process in hot water bath, following canning directions on page 186.

Yields: 6 to 7 half pints.

Did You Know? . . . .

Did you know that blueberry production in North America typically starts in mid May (in Florida) and ends in September, when some fruit is held over in controlled-atmosphere storage in Oregon, Washington, and Canada?

Orange Blueberry Freezer Jam

While it is nice to eat berries fresh when they are in season, by making jam you will be able to savor their flavor year round.

Ingredients:

2½ c. sugar
1   med. orange
1½ c. fresh blueberries, mashed
1   pouch liquid fruit pectin

Directions:

1. Preheat oven to 250 degrees F.
2. Place sugar in shallow baking dish; bake for 15 minutes.
3. Meanwhile, grate 1 tablespoon peel from orange, making sure to grate only outside of peel (white pith makes peel bitter).
4. Peel, segment, and chop orange.
5. In large bowl combine peel, chopped orange, blueberries, and sugar; let stand for 10 minutes stirring occasionally.
6. Add pectin; continue cooking, stirring constantly, for 3 minutes.
7. Ladle into clean jars or freezer containers.
8. Let stand for 24 hours at room temperature.
9. Refrigerate for up to 3 weeks, or freeze for longer storage.

Yields: 4 cups.

Did You Know? . . . .

Did you know that blueberries are sometimes mistakenly called huckleberries?

Easy Blueberry Syrup

Nothing is better than hot pancakes, waffles, or French toast and homemade blueberry syrup. Adjust the sweetness to your taste. I think it is best not too sweet.

Ingredients:

2½ c. frozen blueberries, thawed, with juice
1 c. sugar
1 c. light corn syrup

Directions:

1. Put blueberries (including juice) and sugar in blender, and process at high speed.
2. Pour into saucepan, and bring to a boil over moderate heat.
3. Add corn syrup, and cook a little while longer.
4. Pour into bottle and refrigerate.

Blueberries in Spiced Maple Syrup

For those of you who enjoy spices, this recipe adds a fragrant touch to fresh blueberries. Try using this syrup over vanilla or coffee-flavored ice cream.

Ingredients:

¼ c. maple syrup
½ c. brown sugar, firmly packed
½ c. water
3 strips pared orange peel (about 6 in. long)
1 stick cinnamon
1 Tbs. vanilla extract
4 c. fresh blueberries

Directions:

1. Combine maple syrup, brown sugar, water, orange peel, and cinnamon in saucepan.
2. Cook, covered, over low heat until sugar is completely dissolved, stirring constantly.
3. Add vanilla and blueberries.
4. Simmer slowly until berries are soft but not mushy, stirring carefully.
5. Remove from heat and cool.
6. Remove orange peel and cinnamon and serve.

Spiced Blueberry Jam

Some people enjoy the addition of spices to their jam. Try this version with cinnamon and ginger.

Ingredients:

5   c. blueberries
1½ Tbs. lemon juice
1   pkg. fruit pectin
1   tsp. ground cinnamon
½   tsp. ground ginger
4   c. sugar

Directions:

1. Place blueberries in blender and process at low speed.
2. Transfer into heavy pot.
3. Stir in lemon juice, pectin, and spices; bring to rolling boil, stirring constantly.
4. Add sugar, bring to boil again, and boil for 1 minute.
5. Remove from heat, skim off foam, and ladle into sterilized hot jars.
6. Process in hot water bath, following canning directions on page 186.

Blueberry Syrup

Try this delicious version of syrup. It is full of true blueberry flavor. While this recipe normally gives good results, fruit sugar, pectin, and acid concentrations can vary. Start with a small test batch, and allow it to cool thoroughly before testing for syrup thickness.

Ingredients:

    2   c. blueberry juice
    1¾ c. sugar
    1   Tbs. lemon juice (optional) for tarter syrup

Directions:

1. Crush fruit; press out juice using cheesecloth or jelly bag.
2. If you will not be making syrup immediately, pasteurize juice by heating to 194 degrees F. for 1 minute; filter through cheesecloth and refrigerate.
3. Mix juice and sugar in large pan, and bring to rolling boil; continue to boil for 1 minute.
4. Remove pan from heat and skim off any foam.
5. Pour syrup into clean, hot canning jars.
6. Process following canning directions on page 186.
7. Refrigerate after opening.
8. This recipe produces fairly thin syrup. If you desire thicker syrup, use 1½ cups sugar and ¼ cup corn syrup in recipe.
9. Do not add more sugar or boil longer to thicken, because both methods can cause jelling to occur.
10. Corn syrup and lemon juice can be used together.

Did You Know? . . . .

Did you know that feeding blueberries to animals lowers stroke damage?

Blueberry Jam with Sherry

This version of blueberry jam adds the flavor of orange and sherry for a delicious spread.

Ingredients:

    ½ gal. blueberries
    2 boxes fruit pectin
    2 pieces orange peel (4-in. lengths)
    7 c. sugar
    1 c. sherry
      juice from 2 oranges

Directions:

1. Wash and drain berries.
2. In blender liquefy all but 1 cup blueberries together with orange juice.
3. Pour into 6- to 8-quart pot.
4. Add remaining whole berries and stir in fruit pectin.
5. Add orange peel, and bring to rolling boil over medium-high heat, stirring constantly.
6. Add sugar and sherry.
7. Bring to boil again and cook 1 minute longer.
8. Remove from heat, skim off foam, and remove orange peel.
9. Ladle into hot jars, and process in hot water bath, following canning directions on page 186.

Yields: 8 jars (12 ounces each).

Did You Know?....

Did you know that you should not wash berries until just before using to prevent berries from becoming mushy?

Tart Blueberry Butter

Use this simple blueberry butter on English muffins, pancakes, or crepes.

Ingredients:

    1 c. blended blueberries (whip berries in food
       processor or blender until smooth)

Directions:

1. Heat blended blueberries to a boil in saucepan.
2. Turn heat to low and simmer, stirring occasionally, until mixture reaches desired thickness.

Yields: ⅓ cup.

No-Cook Blueberry Strawberry Jam

What can be easier than a jam that you do not have to cook or can?

Ingredients:

    1 c. strawberries, crushed
    2 c. blueberries, fresh or frozen, crushed
    5 c. sugar
    2 Tbs. lemon juice
    2 pouches liquid pectin

Directions:

1. Measure prepared fruit into large bowl.
2. Add sugar to fruit and mix well; let stand for 10 minutes.
3. Stir in lemon juice and pectin.
4. Continue to stir for 3 minutes until most of the sugar is dissolved.

5. Pour into clean jars or plastic containers, and cover tightly with lids.
6. Let stand at room temperature until set, up to 24 hours.
7. Store in freezer or up to 3 weeks in refrigerator.

Yields: 7 cups.

Blueberry Blackberry Spice Syrup

The combination of blueberries and blackberries in this spicy syrup makes it a tasty treat on pancakes or waffles.

Ingredients:

10 oz. blueberries (2 c.)
12 oz. blackberries (2½ c.)
1 c. sugar
½ c. water
1 cinnamon stick (3-in. length)
1 whole clove
1 green cardamom pod (optional)
1 pinch salt

Directions:

1. Bring berries, sugar, water, spices, and salt to a boil in heavy, medium saucepan, stirring until sugar is dissolved.
2. Reduce heat and simmer, uncovered, stirring occasionally until fruit is very soft, about 30 minutes.
3. Strain through fine-mesh sieve into bowl, pressing gently on and then discarding solids.
4. Cool, then chill, covered.

Yields: About 1¾ cups.

Speedy Blueberry Refrigerator Jam

This jam can be made very quickly. That is very handy on a busy day.

Ingredients:

- 4 c. blueberries, fresh or frozen
- 2 c. sugar
- 3 oz. lemon-flavored gelatin

Directions:

1. In large saucepan combine all three ingredients.
2. Bring to a boil; cook and stir for 2 minutes.
3. Pour into jars; refrigerate.

Yields: 3 cups.

Wild Blueberry Lemon Jam

This is another flavorful jam to enjoy.

Ingredients:

- 5 c. frozen wild blueberries, thawed
- 1 pkg. dry pectin
- 5 c. sugar
- 1 Tbs. grated lemon zest
- ⅓ c. lemon juice

Ingredients:

1. Crush thawed wild blueberries one layer at a time, or chop frozen in food processor.
2. Combine blueberries and pectin in large saucepot.
3. Bring to a boil, stirring frequently.
4. Add sugar, stirring until dissolved.

5. Stir in grated lemon peel and lemon juice.
6. Return to a rolling boil, and boil hard 1 minute, stirring constantly.
7. Remove from heat; skim foam if necessary.
8. Ladle hot jam into hot jars, leaving ¼-inch headspace; adjust two-piece caps.
9. Process 15 minutes in a boiling water canner, following canning directions on page 186.

Yields: About 8 half pints.

Blueberry Jelly

For those of you who prefer clear jelly over jam, try this recipe.

Ingredients:

5½ c. blueberry juice (recipe page 252)
2   Tbs. lemon juice
2   pkg. fruit pectin
8   c. sugar
½   tsp. almond extract

Directions:

1. Combine blueberry juice, lemon juice, and powdered pectin in large pan.
2. Bring to rolling boil over medium-high heat, stirring constantly.
3. Add sugar all at once, and continue stirring until mixture comes to a full boil again.
4. Allow to boil 1 minute, and then remove from heat.
5. Stir in almond extract, skim off foam, ladle into jars, and process in hot water bath, following canning directions on page 186.

Yields: About 5 pints.

Apple Butter with Blueberries

This apple-blueberry butter is great warm or chilled, especially on pancakes or sourdough toast.

Ingredients:

    1 lb. cooking apples (about 6 med.)
    ½ c. blueberries
    1 Tbs. apple cider
    1 Tbs. fresh lemon juice
    ¼ tsp. ground cinnamon
    1 Tbs. unsalted butter

Directions:

1. Peel, core, and thinly slice apples.
2. Combine apple slices, blueberries, cider, lemon juice, and cinnamon in 1-quart casserole dish and cover.
3. Microwave on full power until fruit is very tender, about 10 minutes.
4. Uncover and let mixture cool for about 5 minutes.
5. Combine fruit mixture (including liquids) and butter in processor or blender, and process until puréed, about 5 seconds.
6. Stores covered and refrigerated for up to a week.

Yields: 1½ cups.

Did You Know? . . . .

Did you know that blueberries were first cultivated in the United States by Elizabeth Coleman White in the South Jersey village of Whitesbog?

Blueberry Delights Cookbook

A Collection of Blueberry Recipes
Cookbook Delights Series-Book 2

Main Dishes

Table of Contents

Did You Know? . . . .

Did you know that blueberries can be distinguished from bilberries by cutting them in half? Ripe blueberries have white or greenish flesh, while bilberries and huckleberries are colored purple throughout.

Beef Medallions with Blueberry Citrus Sauce

Beef medallions make an elegant dinner presentation. Try serving these blueberry medallions with your favorite potato, pasta, or rice.

Ingredients:

    1 c. blueberries, fresh or frozen
    6 Tbs. orange juice
    6 Tbs. lemon juice
    2 Tbs. vermouth
    2 tsp. grated orange peel
    2 tsp. grated lemon peel
    1 tsp. minced fresh ginger
    1 Tbs. butter
    1 lb. beef medallions
    salt and pepper to taste

Directions:

1. Combine blueberries, orange juice, lemon juice, vermouth, orange peel, lemon peel, and ginger; stir to blend and set aside.
2. Melt butter in large, heavy skillet; sauté beef until brown and just cooked through.
3. Transfer beef to platter and keep warm.
4. Add blueberry mixture to skillet, and cook until mixture thickens, about 2 minutes.
5. Spoon blueberry mixture over beef and serve.

Did You Know? . . . .

Did you know that chilling berries soon after picking increases shelf life? If refrigerated, fresh-picked blueberries will keep 10 to 14 days.

Salmon with Blueberry Horseradish Sauce

Northwest salmon, blueberries, and horseradish combine to make a piquant Northwest dish.

Ingredients:

    1 lb. salmon fillet
    ½ c. water
    1 pt. fresh blueberries
    ½ c. sugar
    1 oz. freshly grated horseradish
    ½ c. fresh basil
       juice of ½ lemon

Directions:

1. Cut salmon into 6 pieces (2 ounces each), and poach until just underdone or internal temperature reaches 125 degrees F.
2. Cool immediately in refrigerator.
3. Bring water to a boil and add blueberries; reduce heat and simmer just until tender.
4. Add sugar, and cook for just a few more minutes.
5. Finish with lemon juice and grated horseradish.
6. Stir in basil after cooking.
7. Serve warm, pooled on a plate with chilled salmon on top.
8. Garnish with sprig of basil.

Did You Know? . . . .

Did you know that the blueberry is one of the few fruits that is native to North America (along with cranberries and Concord grapes)?

Pastrami-Spiced Beef with Blueberry Sauce

My family enjoys a spiced beef, and this marinated version is excellent served with blueberry sauce. Remember that the trick is to serve the meat rich in spices.

Ingredients for beef:

2	Tbs. coriander seeds
2	Tbs. mustard seeds
2	Tbs. white peppercorns
2	Tbs. allspice berries
6-8	dried red chilies
1	piece dried gingerroot (2-in. length)
1	piece cinnamon stick (2-in. length)
6	dried bay leaves
4	Tbs. kosher salt
1	c. blueberries
4	Tbs. sugar
1	beef loin (4 lb.), trimmed of excess fat
4	c. vegetable oil
	blueberry sauce (recipe follows)

Ingredients for blueberry sauce:

2	Tbs. vegetable oil
1	lg. garlic clove, crushed
1	Tbs. minced fresh ginger
1	med. onion, finely chopped
2	pt. blueberries
1	c. fresh tomato, peeled, seeded, chopped
2	lg. purple plums, pitted, chopped
¼	c. dark brown sugar, firmly packed
1	Tbs. blueberry vinegar (recipe page 188)
1	Tbs. fresh lemon juice
1	med. dried chili pepper, crumbled

1   tsp. ground cinnamon
1   tsp. ground cardamom
1   tsp. ground coriander
1   tsp. salt
1   tsp. freshly ground mixed peppercorns
    zest of 1 lemon, cut into julienne strips

Directions for beef:

1. In spice mill or with mortar and pestle, grind spices, blueberries, and sugar into paste, working in batches as necessary; combine batches of spices in small bowl.
2. Place beef loin on sheet of plastic wrap, and rub on all sides with pastrami-spice paste; wrap tightly in plastic wrap to marinate.
3. Refrigerate wrapped loin for at least 12 hours and up to 24 hours.
4. Preheat oven to 400 degrees F.
5. In large sauté or roasting pan, heat vegetable oil over high heat.
6. Add beef to pan, and sear quickly on all sides, being careful not to burn spices.
7. Place seared beef in oven, and bake about 45 minutes or until thermometer inserted into center reads 142 degrees F.
8. Remove loin from oven; cover and let rest for 15 minutes.
9. Carve and serve with blueberry sauce.

Directions for blueberry sauce:

1. Heat oil in heavy-bottom, 2-quart saucepan; add garlic and ginger, and cook over low heat for 2 minutes.
2. Add onion; cook until soft and transparent, stirring often.

3. Add blueberries, tomato, plums, brown sugar, vinegar, lemon juice, zest, chili pepper, spices, salt, and pepper; stir well.
4. Cook over medium heat until mixture begins to simmer.
5. Reduce heat; continue simmering gently for 30 minutes.
6. Remove from heat and let mixture cool slightly; purée in food processor or blender.
7. Return purée to pan and heat, bringing mixture to a simmer; cook until thick, about 1 hour.
8. Pour amount not using into sterile half-pint jars or containers; cover and let cool.
9. Store in refrigerator for up to 4 weeks, or freeze up to 4 months.

Yields: 6 servings.

Blueberry Filling for Pierogies

Blueberries make a great filling for old-fashioned pierogies.

Ingredients:
    4 c. fresh blueberries
    3 tsp. sugar

Directions:
1. Wash berries and drain.
2. In medium bowl sprinkle berries with sugar.
3. Mix lightly.
4. Fill pierogi shells and process immediately, before juice is drawn out of fruit.

Yields: 4 cups, enough for 40 to 45 pierogies.

Blueberry Chicken Breast

This is another tasty and colorful chicken dish. Remember the importance of reducing the liquids in the sauce to obtain the full flavor of the ingredients.

Ingredients:

    4 boneless, skinless chicken breast halves
    ½ tsp. Cajun spices or to taste
    3 tsp. olive oil
    3 cloves garlic, finely chopped
    1 med. onion, finely chopped
    ½ c. red wine
    2 c. blueberries
       grated rind of 1 lemon
       salt and pepper to taste

Directions:

1. Dust chicken breasts with Cajun spices.
2. Sauté in olive oil until brown and almost cooked through, 7 to 10 minutes.
3. Remove chicken breasts from pan and keep warm.
4. In same pan sauté garlic and onion until transparent, scraping remaining bits of chicken from bottom of pan.
5. Add red wine, blueberries, and lemon rind; cook down, about 5 minutes, until most of liquid is evaporated.
6. Add salt and pepper to taste; let sit for 5 minutes, heat off, for flavors to blend.
7. Spoon over reserved chicken breasts and serve.

Roasted Chicken with Blueberry Sauce

This makes a delicious and colorful main dish, and the trick is to make sure you reduce the stock to concentrate the flavor.

Ingredients:

- 2   c. port wine
- 2   c. water
- ¾   c. sugar, divided
- ¼   c. honey
- 1   whole chicken (4 lb.), wing tips removed
- 2   Tbs. olive oil
- ⅓   c. diced shallots
- ½   c. cider vinegar
- ¼   c. brandy
- 1   c. fresh blueberries
- 1½ tsp. chopped fresh tarragon
- 2   c. chicken stock
  salt and ground black pepper
  fresh blueberries for garnish
  carrot rosettes for garnish

Directions:

1. In pot large enough to hold chicken, combine port, water, ¼ cup sugar, and honey; bring to a boil.
2. Meanwhile, season chicken cavity with salt and black pepper; truss chicken and set aside.
3. When wine mixture comes to a boil, remove from heat.
4. Add chicken; let marinate at room temperature for 30 minutes, turning occasionally.
5. Preheat oven to 350 degrees F.
6. Remove chicken from marinade; place on rack in shallow roasting pan.

7. Bake for about 1 hour and 15 minutes or until chicken is brown and reaches internal temperature of 185 degrees F.
8. Remove from oven and let stand at room temperature for 10 minutes.
9. While chicken is baking, in medium skillet heat olive oil until hot.
10. Add shallots; cook, stirring frequently, until soft, 3 to 5 minutes.
11. Add remaining ½ cup sugar; cook over low heat, stirring frequently, until sugar is dark brown, 10 to 15 minutes.
12. Stir in vinegar, brandy, blueberries, and tarragon.
13. Cook over medium-high heat until blueberries are soft, about 5 minutes.
14. Add chicken stock; bring to a boil, and boil until reduced by half, about 20 minutes.
15. Season to taste with salt and pepper.
16. To serve, carve chicken, dividing among serving plates.
17. Spoon blueberry sauce over chicken.
18. Garnish with fresh blueberries, carrot rosettes, etc., if desired.

Yields: 2 to 4 servings with 1½ cups sauce.

Did You Know? . . . .

Did you know that the easiest and fastest way to pick blueberries is to hold your bucket under them in one hand, and with your other hand, cup a ripe bunch and gently rub them with your fingers? The ripe berries will drop into your bucket, while the unripe ones will remain attached to the bush.

Sour Cream Soufflé with Blueberries

Try this interesting soufflé. The Parmesan cheese and sour cream cut the sweetness and are a great contrast to the sweet blueberry.

Ingredients:

> 6 lg. egg yolks
> ½ c. sour cream
> ¼ c. grated Parmesan cheese
> 6 egg whites, stiffly beaten
> 3 Tbs. butter
> ½ c. sour cream sweetened with 1 tsp. sugar or to taste
> fresh blueberries

Directions:

1. Preheat oven to 325 degrees F.
2. Beat egg yolks until thick and pale colored, about 5 minutes.
3. Mix together sour cream and Parmesan cheese; add ½ cup egg yolks.
4. Fold in stiffly beaten egg whites.
5. Melt butter in 10-inch cast iron skillet.
6. Scrape in egg mixture, leveling gently.
7. Cook over very low heat for 10 minutes, uncovered.
8. Carefully move to oven and bake for 15 minutes, until golden and puffed.
9. Cut into 4 wedges, and serve in pan at the table.
10. Top each serving with dollop of sweetened sour cream, and sprinkle with fresh berries.

Yields: 4 servings.

Trout with Blueberries

I grew up in Montana where we frequently enjoyed fresh trout. This is very easy to make grilled or baked. Feel free to use salmon with the same recipe.

Ingredients:

    2 tsp. butter, divided
    1 lemon, sliced
    1 whole trout, cleaned, or center-cut trout of choice
    1 c. blueberries
    ½ onion, chopped

Directions:

1. Spread 1 tsp. butter around center of aluminum foil, arrange half of lemon slices over butter, and place trout on top.
2. Mix together berries and onion; stuff fish.
3. Spread remaining butter on top of trout, arrange remaining lemon slices over top, then fold and seal foil.
4. Grill 10 minutes per inch of trout at thickest point, turning every 5 to 10 minutes.
5. Unwrap foil, peel off skin, and remove bones.
6. Place trout fillets on plates; spoon stuffing and lemon slices on top.
7. Note: Substitute covered dish in place of foil, and bake in preheated oven at 350 degrees F. for 10 minutes per inch; follow same approach to serving.

Did You Know? . . . .

Did you know that blueberries are ranked No. 1 in antioxidant activity compared with 40 other commercially available fruits and vegetables?

Blueberry-Stuffed Cornish Game Hens

Cornish game hens are always a treat. The blueberry stuffing in this recipe makes them especially flavorful.

Ingredients:

  8 Cornish game hens, thawed
  ¼ c. oil
  ¼ c. lemon juice
  ¼ c. Angostura bitters
  4 c. fresh blueberries
  4 tsp. sugar
  ½ c. butter, softened
  8 small bay leaves
     salt and pepper

Directions:

  1. Preheat oven to 350 degrees F.
  2. Sprinkle game hens inside and out with salt and pepper.
  3. Mix oil, lemon juice, and Angostura bitters; brush game hens with mixture inside and out.
  4. Fill each bird with ½ cup blueberries and ½ teaspoon sugar.
  5. Sew or skewer opening and place in shallow roasting pan.
  6. Spread soft butter over breasts of birds, and place bay leaf on butter.
  7. Roast for 1 hour or until leg is easily moved.

Yields: 8 servings.

Did You Know?....

Did you know that in the United States, July is National Blueberry Month?

Chicken Grill with Tangy Blueberry Sauce

This chicken can be prepared by grilling or using the broiler, microwave, or pan sauté methods. Raspberry vinegar may be substituted for the blueberry vinegar.

Ingredients:

  3   Tbs. olive oil
  3   Tbs. blueberry vinegar (recipe page 188)
  1½ tsp. lime juice
  2   cloves garlic, minced
  4   chicken breast halves, skin removed
  1   c. blueberries
  1   c. puréed raspberries

Directions:

1. In nonreactive dish or sturdy plastic zip-closure bag, combine oil, vinegar, lime juice, and garlic.
2. Add chicken, turning to coat all sides; marinate in refrigerator for 1 to 2 hours.
3. Reserving marinade, remove chicken and pat dry with paper towel.
4. Prepare sauce by combining marinade, blueberries, and raspberry purée in saucepan.
5. Stirring occasionally, place over medium heat and cook 5 to 7 minutes, until slightly thickened.
6. Remove from heat and set aside.
7. Serve chicken with blueberry-raspberry sauce.
8. To grill chicken, place over medium heat, cooking 8 to 12 minutes per side or until juices are no longer pink when chicken is cut to the bone.

Yields: 4 servings.

Chicken Satay with Wild Blueberry Peanut Butter Sauce

If you want to make a hot blueberry peanut butter sauce, add hot peppers or hot red pepper sauce to this recipe.

Ingredients for sauce:

3	Tbs. finely chopped or grated fresh ginger
1	shallot or ¼ c. onion
1	tsp. oil
6	oz. water
3	Tbs. crunchy peanut butter
1½ c. frozen wild blueberries
1	tsp. cornstarch
½	tsp. salt

Ingredients for chicken:

2	double chicken breasts (or 4 single) or 1 lb. pre-packaged, thinly sliced chicken breast
1	Tbs. olive oil
	salt and pepper
	skewers

Directions for sauce:

1. Peel shallot and finely dice.
2. Heat oil and briefly sauté ginger and shallot.
3. Add water and peanut butter over medium heat and whisk together.
4. Add frozen wild blueberries.
5. Mix small amount of water in cornstarch, and add to berry/peanut butter sauce.
6. Bring to a boil, and simmer for about 3 minutes.
7. Season to taste with salt and pepper.

Directions for chicken:

1. Cut chicken breast fillets lengthwise into thin strips, or use prepared sliced breasts.

2. Flavor with salt and pepper.
3. Put strips in an accordion manner onto lightly oiled skewers.
4. Heat oil in coated pan, and cook skewers on both sides for 2 to 3 minutes each.
5. Serve with blueberry sauce.
6. Note: To cook chicken off skewers, cut chicken in bite-size pieces, sauté, and serve with toothpicks on a platter with bowl of sauce for dipping.

Yields: 4 servings.

Wild Blueberry Rhubarb Pork Chops

This is a delicious way to use some of your rhubarb.

Ingredients:
   4 pork chops (about 5 oz. each)
   2 c. chopped rhubarb
   2 c. wild blueberries
   2 Tbs. honey
   2 Tbs. brown sugar, firmly packed
   ⅛ tsp. ground cinnamon
   ¼ c. all-purpose flour
      salt and pepper to taste
      cooking spray

Directions:
1. Dredge chops in flour, salt, and pepper to coat.
2. Spray skillet with cooking spray, and brown chops.
3. Mix rhubarb, berries, honey, brown sugar, and cinnamon; add to chops in skillet.
4. Cook on medium-low heat for 20 to 30 minutes.

Yields: 4 servings.

Berry Pretty Pork Roast

This moist roast is particularly tasty when served with the cooking juices.

Ingredients:

    1 boneless, whole pork loin roast (about 2½ lb.)
    ½ c. chopped dried plums
    ⅓ c. blueberries, fresh or frozen
    ⅓ c. raspberries, fresh or frozen
    ⅓ c. strawberries, fresh or frozen, sliced
    2 cloves garlic, cut into slivers
    ¼ c. butter, melted
    ½ tsp. dried oregano
    ¼ tsp. salt
    ¼ tsp. pepper
    ½ c. red wine or chicken broth
    1 Tbs. brown sugar
    1 Tbs. seedless raspberry jam

Directions:

1. Preheat oven to 350 degrees F.
2. Make lengthwise slit down center of roast to within ½ inch of bottom.
3. Open roast so it lies flat, and cover with plastic wrap.
4. Flatten to ¾-inch thickness, and then remove plastic.
5. Combine fruit; place on one side of roast.
6. Close roast; tie several times with kitchen string, securing ends with toothpicks.
7. Cut slits in roasts; insert garlic slivers.
8. Place in ungreased shallow baking pan.
9. Drizzle with butter, and then sprinkle with oregano, salt, and pepper.
10. In small bowl combine wine or broth, brown sugar, and jam; drizzle over roast.
11. Bake uncovered for 75 to 80 minutes or until meat thermometer reaches 160 degrees F.
12. Let stand for 10 minutes before slicing.

Yields: 8 to 10 servings.

Blueberry Delights Cookbook

A Collection of Blueberry Recipes
Cookbook Delights Series-Book 2

Pies

Table of Contents

Page

Did You Know? . . . .

Did you know that Native Americans in the Northwest Territory smoked wild blueberries to preserve them for the winter?

A Basic Recipe for Pie Crust

This is a very good recipe for a delicious, flaky crust.

Ingredients for single crust:

1½ c. sifted all-purpose flour
½   tsp. salt
½   c. shortening
4-5 Tbs. ice water

Ingredients for double crust:

2   c. sifted all-purpose flour
1   tsp. salt
⅔   c. shortening
5-7 Tbs. ice water

Directions for single crust:

1. In large bowl stir together flour and salt.
2. Cut in shortening with pastry blender or mix with fingertips until pieces are size of coarse crumbs.
3. Sprinkle 2 tablespoons ice water over flour mixture, tossing with fork.
4. Add just enough remaining water 1 tablespoon at a time to moisten dough, tossing so dough holds together.
5. Roll pastry into 11-inch circle and wrap in plastic wrap; refrigerate for 1 hour.
6. Preheat oven to 425 degrees F.
7. Remove plastic wrap from pastry, and fit pastry into a 9-inch pie plate.
8. Fold edge under, then crimp between thumb and forefinger to make fluted crust.
9. For filled pie with an instant or cooked filling (cream-filled, custard-filled, etc.), prick crust all over with fork then bake 15 to 20 minutes until done.
10. If preparing pie with uncooked filling (such as pumpkin), do not prick crust; pour filling into unbaked pastry shell, and then bake as directed.

Directions for double crust:

1. Turn desired filling into pastry-lined pie plate; trim overhanging edge of pastry ½ inch from rim of plate.
2. Cut slits with knife in top crust for steam vents.
3. Place over filling; trim overhanging edge of pastry 1 inch from rim of plate.
4. Fold and roll top edge under lower edge, pressing on rim to seal; flute.
5. Cover fluted edge with 2- to 3-inch-wide strip of aluminum foil to prevent excessive browning.
6. Remove foil during last 15 minutes of baking.

Yields: 1 pie crust (9-inch single or double).

A Basic Cookie or Graham Cracker Crust

This is a great crust for use with cream pies or for an unbaked pie. Use your favorite flavor of cookie to complement your filling, or use graham crackers.

Ingredients:

2 c. cookie or graham cracker crumbs, finely crushed
⅓ c. sugar
½ c. butter, melted

Directions:

1. Combine crumbs, sugar, and butter.
2. Press mixture firmly against bottom and up sides of 9-inch pie plate.
3. Baking is not necessary, but if preferred crust may be baked at 400 degrees F. for 10 minutes.

Yields: 1 pie crust (9-inch).

Blueberry Coconut Pie

This blueberry pie keeps well in your freezer for surprise guests or for your invited company.

Ingredients:

- 1   single-crust 9-inch pastry shell (recipe page 224)
- 1   egg, well beaten
- 1¼ c. flaked coconut
- ¼   c. chopped walnuts
- ¼   c. light corn syrup
- 1   Tbs. all-purpose flour
- ¼   tsp. salt
- ¼   c. plus ⅔ c. sugar, divided
- 1   pkg. frozen blueberries (10 oz.), unsweetened
- 1   c. heavy cream, whipped

Directions:

1. Make pastry shell, and bake as directed except remove it from oven after only 5 minutes of baking; reduce oven temperature to 375 degrees F.
2. Combine egg with coconut, nuts, syrup, flour, salt, and ¼ cup sugar; spread in bottom of partly baked pastry shell.
3. Return pie to oven and bake for 15 minutes; cool thoroughly.
4. Crush frozen blueberries, and combine with remaining ⅔ cup sugar; fold into whipped cream.
5. Pour berry mixture over cooled coconut mixture and freeze.

Yields: 6 servings.

Blueberry Cream Pie

This is a refreshing and attractive chilled blueberry pie.

Ingredients:

- 1 single-crust 9-inch pastry shell, baked (recipe page 218)
- 3 oz. cream cheese, softened
- ½ c. confectioners' sugar
- 1 tsp. vanilla extract
- 2 c. fresh blueberries
- 1 c. sugar
- ½ c. water
- 3 Tbs. cornstarch
- 1 c. whipping cream
  blueberries for garnish

Directions:

1. Prepare pastry shell; cool.
2. Mix cream cheese, confectioners' sugar, and vanilla together.
3. Spread cream mixture onto bottom of pie shell.
4. In saucepan combine blueberries, sugar, water, and cornstarch.
5. Bring to a boil, stirring constantly; cook until thickened.
6. Pour over cream mixture in pie shell; cool.
7. Whip cream and spread on top of cooled pie.
8. Top with fresh blueberries.

Yields: 6 to 8 servings.

Did You Know? . . . .

Did you know that the Northern Highbush Blueberry is the state fruit of New Jersey?

Latticed Blueberry Pie

The lattice top makes this an attractive blueberry pie. There are no spices added to this recipe, so you can enjoy the taste of pure blueberries.

Ingredients:

- 6 c. blueberries
- 1 tsp. almond extract
- 3½ Tbs. all-purpose flour
- 1¼ c. sugar
- ½ tsp. salt
- pastry for double-crust pie (recipe page 224)

Directions:

1. Preheat oven to 375 degrees F.
2. Prepare pastry; line pie pan with crust and set aside.
3. Sprinkle extract over berries.
4. Mix flour, sugar, and salt; combine with blueberries, and transfer to crust-lined pie pan.
5. Roll out second crust, and cut strips about ½ inch wide with pastry wheel or knife.
6. Place ½ of strips horizontally over filling.
7. Lay second set of strips vertically across first layer; weave strips if desired.
8. Trim ends of strips; fold and flute edge of pie, building a higher crust to prevent filling from bubbling over.
9. Loosely cover with foil.
10. Bake for about 20 minutes; remove foil and bake another 25 minutes.
11. Allow to cool on wire rack before slicing to serve.

Yields: 6 to 8 servings.

Wild Blueberry Pie

This is a very good blueberry pie that is not quite as sweet as some. This recipe uses tapioca as a thickening agent. It is good to try all versions of a pie to see which one you like the best.

Ingredients:

    6 c. wild blueberries, fresh or frozen
    3 Tbs. tapioca
    ⅔ c. sugar
    ½ c. brown sugar, firmly packed
    1 Tbs. cider vinegar
    1 Tbs. butter
    pastry for double-crust pie (recipe page 224)

Directions:

1. Preheat oven to 400 degrees F.
2. Prepare pastry; line pie pan with crust and set aside.
3. Mix together blueberries, tapioca, sugar, brown sugar, and vinegar.
4. Pour mixture into unbaked pie shell.
5. Dot top with butter.
6. Roll out remaining pastry to fit top of pie; cut slits in top, place over filling, and seal and flute edges.
7. Bake for 15 minutes, then turn oven down to 350 degrees F., and bake for 45 to 55 minutes (longer if berries are frozen).

Yields: 6 to 8 servings.

Did You Know? . . . .

Did you know that the "Jersey" is the most planted blueberry in Michigan?

Four-Fruit Pie

The four different fruits in this pie make a very tasty, colorful combination.

Ingredients:

- 1 c. rhubarb, sliced in 1-in. pieces
- 1 c. peeled, chopped apple
- 1 c. blueberries
- 1 c. raspberries
- 1 tsp. lemon juice
- ¾ c. sugar
- ¼ c. all-purpose flour
- 2 Tbs. butter
- pastry for double-crust 9-in. pie (recipe page 224)
- additional sugar (optional)

Directions:

1. Preheat oven to 400 degrees F.
2. In large bowl gently toss rhubarb, apple, berries, and lemon juice.
3. Combine sugar and flour; stir into fruit and let stand for 30 minutes.
4. Line pie plate with bottom crust; add filling and dot with butter.
5. Roll out remaining pastry to fit top of pie; cut slits in top, place over filling, and seal and flute edges.
6. Bake for 50 to 60 minutes or until crust is golden brown and filling is bubbly.
7. Sprinkle with sugar if desired.

Yields: 6 to 8 servings.

Dutch Apple Berry Pie

This pie is a combination of apples and fresh berries with a crumb topping. It is excellent when still warm and topped with whipped cream or ice cream.

Ingredients:

2 c. sliced green apples
½ c. raspberries
½ c. fresh blueberries
⅔ c. all-purpose flour
⅔ c. brown sugar, firmly packed
⅓ c. butter, cut into ½-in. cubes
½ tsp. ground cinnamon
½ tsp. ground allspice
1 pinch ground nutmeg
pastry for 9-in. deep dish pie (recipe page 224)

Directions:

1. Preheat oven to 350 degrees F.
2. Prepare pastry; line pie pan with crust and set aside.
3. Mix apples, raspberries, and blueberries together; pour into pie shell.
4. In medium bowl combine flour, brown sugar, butter, cinnamon, allspice, and nutmeg.
5. Mix until dry and crumbly; sprinkle over fruit.
6. Bake for 30 minutes or until topping is brown.
7. Serve warm topped with whipped cream or ice cream.

Yields: 6 to 8 servings.

Lemon Meringue Blueberry Pie

Begin making this at least one day ahead. It takes extra work, but it is well worth the effort.

Ingredients for lemon curd and mousse:

    1½ c. sugar
    2¼ tsp. cornstarch
    ¾   c. fresh lemon juice
    9   lg. egg yolks
    ¾   c. unsalted butter, cut into ½-inch cubes
    ½   c. chilled heavy whipping cream

Ingredients for blueberry compote:

    1½ c. fresh blueberries, divided
    3   Tbs. sugar
    ½   tsp. fresh lemon juice
    ¼   tsp. finely grated lemon peel
    1   pinch salt
    1   pinch ground cinnamon
    1   tsp. all-purpose flour
       pastry for single-crust 9-in. pie (recipe page 224)

Ingredients for meringue:

    3   lg. egg whites
    ½   c. sugar

Directions for lemon curd and mousse:

1. Whisk sugar and cornstarch in heavy medium saucepan to blend.
2. Gradually add lemon juice, whisking until cornstarch dissolves.
3. Whisk in yolks, and then add butter.

4. Cook over medium heat until curd thickens and boils, whisking constantly, about 8 minutes.
5. Transfer curd to medium bowl; press plastic wrap directly onto surface of curd.
6. Refrigerate at least 1 day. (Can be prepared 5 days ahead. Keep chilled.)
7. Using electric mixer, beat whipping cream in medium bowl until peaks form.
8. Fold ¾ cup lemon curd into whipped cream ¼ cup at a time.
9. Chill lemon mousse at least 2 hours and up to 6 hours. Keep remaining curd chilled.

Directions for blueberry compote:

1. Combine ¾ cup blueberries, sugar, lemon juice, grated lemon peel, salt, and cinnamon in small saucepan.
2. Stir over medium heat until sugar dissolves, about 4 minutes.
3. Whisk in flour; cook 1 minute.
4. Remove from heat; stir in remaining ¾ cup blueberries.
5. Transfer compote to small bowl; cover and refrigerate at least 2 hours. (Can be prepared 1 day ahead. Keep compote refrigerated.)

Directions for crust and assembly:

1. Position rack in center of oven, and preheat to 375 degrees F.
2. Roll out pie crust on lightly floured surface to 13½-inch round.
3. Transfer crust to 9-inch-diameter glass pie dish; trim overhang to 1 inch.
4. Fold edges under and crimp decoratively; chill 30 minutes.
5. Line crust with foil; fill with dried beans or pie weights.

6. Bake crust until sides are set, about 20 minutes.
7. Remove foil and beans from crust; bake crust until golden and cooked through, piercing with fork if crust bubbles, about 20 minutes longer.
8. Transfer to rack and cool completely.
9. Spread 1½ cups of remaining lemon curd over bottom of crust.
10. Using slotted spoon and leaving most of juices behind, spoon ¾ cup blueberry compote evenly over curd.
11. Drop lemon mousse in dollops over blueberries; spread to cover berries completely.
12. Using slotted spoon, spoon remaining blueberries over mousse.
13. Chill pie while preparing meringue.

Directions for meringue:

1. Whisk egg whites and sugar in large metal bowl to blend.
2. Place bowl over saucepan of simmering water (do not let bottom of bowl touch water); whisk constantly until sugar dissolves and mixture is very warm to touch, about 1½ minutes.
3. Remove bowl from over water.
4. Using electric mixer, beat mixture until thick and fluffy peaks form, about 5 minutes.
5. Spoon dollops of fluffy meringue atop pie, leaving 1-inch plain border to expose some of mousse and blueberries.
6. Using pastry torch, singe meringue until golden. (Can be prepared 6 hours ahead. Cover with cake dome and refrigerate.)
7. Alternatively, spoon meringue into pastry bag fitted with large (about ¾-inch) plain tip, and pipe meringue decoratively over top of pie.

Yields 6 to 8 servings.

Blackberry and Blueberry Pie

Blackberries and blueberries are a wonderful taste combination. This terrific pie can be made in the summer with fresh berries or in the winter with frozen ones.

Ingredients:

¾   c. sugar
⅓   c. all-purpose flour
½   tsp. ground cinnamon
4   c. blueberries, fresh or frozen
1½ c. blackberries, fresh or frozen
1   Tbs. lemon juice
2   Tbs. butter
     pastry for 9-in. double-crust pie (recipe page 224)

Directions:

1. Preheat oven to 425 degrees F.
2. Prepare pastry; line pie pan with crust and set aside.
3. Mix sugar, flour, and cinnamon.
4. Stir in berries to coat.
5. Turn filling into pastry-lined pan.
6. Sprinkle with lemon juice and dot with butter.
7. Roll out remaining pastry to fit top of pie; cut slits in top, place over filling, and seal and flute edges.
8. Cover edges with foil to prevent burning; remove foil for last 12 minutes of baking.
9. Bake for 35 to 45 minutes.

Yields: 6 to 8 servings.

Did You Know? . . . .

Did you know that blueberries are high in dietary fiber, vitamin A, and niacin?

Streusel-Topped Pear and Blueberry Pie

This delicious pie is great when served either slightly warm or at room temperature. Top it with a dollop of sweetened whipped cream.

Ingredients for crust:

- 1½ c. all-purpose flour
- 1 Tbs. sugar
- ¼ tsp. salt
- ½ c. chilled unsalted butter, cut into ½-inch pieces
- 3 Tbs. (or more) ice water

Ingredients for filling:

- 2 lb. firm but ripe pears (about 5 med.), peeled, cored, cut into ¾-inch pieces
- 9 Tbs. sugar, divided
- 2 Tbs. orange juice
- 1 pinch salt
- 2¼ c. frozen blueberries
- 6 Tbs. all-purpose flour

Ingredients for walnut streusel topping:

- 1 c. all-purpose flour
- ½ c. dark brown sugar, firmly packed
- ½ c. walnuts, toasted
- ½ c. chilled unsalted butter, cut into ½-inch pieces
- ¼ tsp. salt

Directions for crust:

1. Blend flour, sugar, and salt in processor.
2. Add chilled butter pieces, and cut in using on/off turns until mixture resembles coarse meal.
3. Add 3 tablespoons ice water, and process until moist clumps form, adding more ice water by teaspoonfuls if dough is dry.

4. Gather dough into ball; flatten into disk.
5. Wrap in plastic and refrigerate 30 minutes. (Can be prepared 2 days ahead. Keep refrigerated. Let soften slightly at room temperature before rolling out.)
6. Roll out dough on lightly floured surface to 12-inch round.
7. Transfer to 9-inch-diameter glass pie dish.
8. Fold edges under, forming high-standing rim ¾ inch above dish sides; crimp edges decoratively.
9. Freeze crust 25 minutes.
10. Preheat oven to 350 degrees F.
11. Bake crust until light golden brown, about 30 minutes.
12. Cool while preparing filling.
13. Maintain oven temperature.

Directions for filling:

1. Combine pear pieces, 3 tablespoons sugar, orange juice, and salt in large nonstick skillet.
2. Cook over medium heat until pears are tender but still hold their shape, stirring often, about 6 minutes.
3. Transfer pear mixture to large bowl; cool to room temperature.
4. Add blueberries, flour, and remaining 6 tablespoons sugar to pears; toss gently to blend.
5. Transfer filling to cooled pie crust, mounding filling slightly in center.
6. Sprinkle with walnut streusel topping.
7. Bake pie until juices bubble thickly, fruit is tender, and streusel topping is golden brown, about 65 minutes.
8. Cool pie on rack until lukewarm.

Directions for walnut streusel topping:

1. Using on/off turns, blend all ingredients in processor until coarse crumbs form.

Yields: 6 to 8 servings; about 2½ cups streusel.

Fresh Blueberry Pie

There is no baking for this pie filling. Fresh berries are piled into the pastry shell, and then topped with cooked berries. After the pie is chilled, serve it with freshly whipped cream for a cool, tasty treat.

Ingredients:

- 1 single-crust 8-in. pastry shell, baked, cooled (recipe page 218)
- 2 pt. fresh blueberries, divided
- 1 Tbs. all-purpose flour
- 1 Tbs. butter
- 1 Tbs. lemon juice
- ½ c. sugar

Directions:

1. Pour 1 pint of blueberries into baked pie shell.
2. In saucepan combine flour, butter, lemon juice, and sugar; mix thoroughly.
3. Add remaining pint of blueberries, and bring just to a boil over medium heat. (Berries should begin to pop open.)
4. Pour cooked berries over fresh berries; chill pie.

Sweetened Whipped Cream

There is nothing as rich and delicious as sweetened whipped cream.

Ingredients:

- 1 c. heavy cream
- ¼ c. sugar
- 1 tsp. vanilla extract

Directions:

1. For best results thoroughly chill cream, bowl, and beaters before whipping.
2. Whip cream until almost stiff.
3. Add sugar and vanilla; beat until cream holds peaks.

Creamy Blueberry Pie

The filling of this pie is a sweet, eggy, sour cream mixture that is spooned over fresh blueberries. Then it is topped with a sweet, buttery crumble. To dress it up, garnish with mint sprigs and additional blueberries.

Ingredients:

 1   single-crust pastry shell, unbaked (recipe page 224)
 1½ c. sugar, divided
 ⅓   c. plus ½ c. all-purpose flour, divided
 ⅛   tsp. salt
 2   eggs, beaten
 ½   c. sour cream
 3   c. fresh blueberries
 ¼   c. butter
     additional blueberries for garnish
     mint leaves for garnish

Directions:

1. Preheat oven to 350 degrees F.
2. Prepare pastry; line 9-inch pie pan with crust, and set aside.
3. Combine 1 cup sugar, ⅓ cup flour, and salt.
4. Add eggs and sour cream, stirring until blended.
5. Place blueberries in pastry shell, and spoon sour cream mixture over berries.
6. In another bowl combine remaining ½ cup sugar and ½ cup flour.
7. Cut in butter with pastry blender until mixture resembles coarse meal.
8. Sprinkle this mixture over sour cream mixture and berries in pie shell.
9. Bake for 50 to 55 minutes or until lightly browned.
10. If desired, garnish with additional blueberries and mint leaves.

Blueberry Cherry Pie

Blueberries and cherries make a great combination in this delicious pie.

Ingredients:

  1¼ c. sugar
  ¼   c. all-purpose flour
  1   Tbs. ground cinnamon
  2   c. pitted cherries
  2   c. blueberries, rinsed, drained
  ½   tsp. lemon juice
  1   Tbs. butter
      pastry for double-crust pie (recipe page 224)

Directions:

  1. Preheat oven to 375 degrees F.
  2. Prepare pastry; line pie pan with crust and set aside.
  3. Mix sugar, flour, and cinnamon in large bowl.
  4. Add fruit, then add lemon juice and stir well.
  5. Pour into prepared pie shell; dot with butter.
  6. Cover with top crust and flute edges; cut small slits in top.
  7. Bake for 1 hour.
  8. Note: Put a baking sheet underneath to catch any liquid that might bubble over.

Yields: 6 to 8 servings.

Did You Know?....

Did you know that Maine's 60,023 acres of blueberries were propagated from native plants that occur naturally in the understory of its coastal forests?

Blueberry Delights Cookbook

A Collection of Blueberry Recipes
Cookbook Delights Series-Book 2

Preserving

Table of Contents

Did You Know? . . . .

*Did you know that you should freeze berries in freezer containers
without washing them to keep the skins from toughening?*

A Basic Guide for Canning, Dehydrating, and Freezing

1. Place empty jars in hot, soapy water. Wash well inside and out with brush or soft cloth.
2. Run your finger around rim of each jar, discarding any that are chipped or cracked.
3. Rinse in clean, clear, very hot water, being careful to use tongs to avoid burning skin or fingers.
4. Place upside down on towel or fabric to drain well.
5. Place lids in boiling water bath for 2 minutes to sterilize and keep hot until ready to place on jar rims.
6. Immediately prior to filling jars with hot food, immerse in hot bath for 1 minute to heat jars. Heating jars avoids breakage.
7. If filling with room-temperature food, you need not immerse immediately prior to filling.
8. Fill jars with food to within ½ inch of neck of jars.
9. When ladling liquid over food, fill jars to within 1 inch of top of rim. This leaves air allowance for sealing purposes.
10. Wipe rims of jars with damp, clean cloth to remove any particles of food and again check for chips or cracks.
11. Using tongs, place lids from hot bath directly onto jars.
12. Place rings over lids, and using cloth, gloves, or holders, tighten down firmly while hanging onto jars.
13. Do not tighten down too hard as air may become trapped in jars and prevent them from sealing.
14. For fruits, tomatoes, and pickled vegetables, place each jar into water bath canning kettle so water covers jars at least 1 inch.
15. For vegetables, process them in a pressure canner according to manufacturer's directions.
16. Follow time recommended for food being canned.
17. Do not mix jars of food in same canning kettle as times may vary for each kind of food.

18. At end of time recommended for canning, gently lift each jar out of bath with tongs, and place on protected surface.
19. Turn lids gently to be sure they are firmly tight.
20. Place filled, ringed jars on cloth to cool gradually.
21. Do not disturb rings, lids, or jars until sealed.
22. Lids will show slight indentation when sealed.
23. When cool, wipe jars with damp cloth then label and date each jar.
24. Leave overnight until thoroughly cooled.
25. Jars may then be stored upright on shelves.

Dehydrating

1. Always begin with fresh, good quality food that is clean and inspected for damage.
2. Pretreatment is not necessary, but food that is blanched will keep its color and flavor better. Use the same blanching times as you would for freezing. Fruit, especially, responds well to pretreatment.
3. Doing some research on pretreatments may help you decide what procedure you would like to use.
4. You can marinate salt, sweeten, or spice foods before you dehydrate them.
5. Jerky is meat that has been marinated and/or flavored by rubbing spices into it; avoid oil or grease of any kind as it will turn rancid as the food dries.
6. Vegetables and fruit can be treated the same way.
7. Slice or dice food thin and uniform so that it will dehydrate evenly. Uneven thicknesses may cause food to spoil because it did not dry as thoroughly as other parts.
8. Space food on dehydrator tray so that air can move around each piece.
9. Try not to let any piece touch another.

10. Fill your trays with all the same type of food as different foods take different amounts of time to dry.

11. You can, of course, dry different types of food at the same time, but you will have to remember to watch and remove the food that dehydrates more quickly. You can mix different foods in the same dehydrator batch, but do not mix strong vegetables like onions and garlic as other foods will absorb their taste while they are dehydrating.

12. The smaller the pieces, the faster a food will dehydrate. Thin leaves of spinach, celery, etc., will dry fastest. Remove them from the stalks before drying them or they will be overdone, losing flavor and quality. In very warm areas, they might even scorch. If they do, they will taste just like burned food when you rehydrate them.

13. Dense food like carrots will feel very hard when they are ready. Others will be crispy. Usually, a food that is high in fructose (sugar) will be leathery when it is finished dehydrating.

14. Remember that food smells when it is in the process of drying, so outdoors or in the garage is an excellent place to dry a big batch of those onions!

15. Always test each batch to make sure it is "done."

16. You can pasteurize finished food by putting it in a slow oven (150 degrees F.) for a few minutes.

17. Let the food cool before storing.

18. Store in airtight containers to guard against moisture. Jars saved from other food work well as long as they have lids that will keep moisture out.

19. Zip-closure food storage bags work well.

20. Jars of dehydrated carrots, celery, beets, etc., may look cheerful on your countertop, but the color and flavor will fade. Dehydrated food keeps its color and flavor best if stored in a dark, cool place.

21. Dehydrating food takes time, so do not rush it. When you are all done, you will have a dried food stash to be proud of!

Freezing

1. Wash all containers and lids in hot, soapy water using soft cloth.
2. Rinse well in clear, clean, hot water.
3. Cool and drain well.
4. Place food into container to within 1 inch of rim. This allows for expansion of food during freezing.
5. Wipe rim of container with clean damp cloth, checking for chips or breaks.
6. Be certain cover fits the container snugly to avoid leaks. Burp air from container.
7. If food is hot when placing in container, cool prior to placing in freezer.
8. Label and date each container.
9. Store upright in freezer until frozen solid.

Canned Blueberries

It is always a good idea to stock up on blueberries when they are in season to enjoy year round.

Ingredients:

    1 gal. fresh blueberries
    4 c. water
    3 c. sugar

Directions:

1. Rinse and drain blueberries.
2. Place in sterilized pint jars.
3. In saucepan bring water and sugar to boil over medium-high heat, stirring constantly.
4. Pour hot mixture over blueberries, leaving ⅜-inch headspace.
5. Process following canning directions on page 236.

Yields: 8 pints.

Blueberry Fruit Leather

My children love all kinds of fruit leather, and blueberry fruit leather makes an extra special treat. Adults will also love this treat.

Ingredients:

    5 c. ripe blueberries
    1½ c. apple juice

Directions:

1. Combine berries and juice in 2-quart saucepan; cook over moderate heat until mixture boils.
2. Lower heat and cook a few minutes longer, until berries are soft.
3. Remove from heat; cool to lukewarm and mash.
4. Strain through fine sieve or double layer of cheesecloth, pressing juice from pulp; discard pulp.
5. Return juice to saucepan and bring to a boil; stir and cook over moderate heat until reduced in volume by half and does not run.
6. Remove from heat and cool; spread 4-inch circles evenly on wax paper-covered cookie sheet.
7. Carefully place in oven at 200 degrees F., and dry 4 to 6 hours with door ajar to reach leather-like consistency; return to oven for additional time if necessary.
8. Or, if using food dehydrator, follow manufacturer's directions.
9. Roll and wrap separately; store in airtight container.

Did You Know? . . . .

Did you know that soldiers in the Civil War regularly drank a blueberry beverage because of its health benefits?

Blueberry Strawberry Fruit Leather

For a little bit different taste, try this fruit leather made with a combination of blueberries and strawberries.

Ingredients:

 4 c. fresh blueberries
 1 c. fresh strawberries
 ¼ c. honey
 1 Tbs. almond extract

Directions:

1. Place blueberries and strawberries in blender or food processor, and process until smooth.
2. Pour mixture through strainer to remove skin and seeds.
3. Stir in honey and almond extract.
4. Place mixture in large skillet (10-inch works best); cook over very low heat for 1 hour until thickened, stirring frequently.
5. Prepare cookie sheet by lining with parchment paper (paper is best but foil can be substituted).
6. Preheat oven to 150 degrees F.
7. Pour thickened mixture onto parchment paper, and spread to form 8 x 12-inch rectangle.
8. Bake for 5½ to 6 hours until fruit sheet is dry enough not to stick to your fingers but moist enough to roll; remove from oven and cool.
9. Once cool, leather should be stored in an airtight container or rolled in plastic wrap.
10. Note: Placing a potholder in oven door to keep it ajar will help dry the leather by allowing moisture to escape.

Yields: 6 pieces (3 x 4 inches each).

Canned Blueberry Pie Filling

This recipe is for one quart of pie filling. Just multiply amounts by however many quarts you desire to make.

Ingredients:

  3½ c. blueberries, fresh or frozen, thawed
  ¾   c. plus 2 Tbs. sugar
  ¼   c. plus 1 Tbs. pectin gel
  1   c. cold water
  ½   c. lemon juice
  3   drops blue food coloring (optional)
  1   drop red food coloring (optional)

Directions:

1. Wash and drain fresh blueberries.
2. For fresh fruit, place 6 cups at a time in 1 gallon boiling water.
3. Boil each batch 1 minute after water returns to a boil.
4. Drain, but keep heated fruit in covered bowl or pot.
5. Combine sugar and pectin gel in large kettle; stir.
6. Add water and, if desired, food coloring.
7. Cook on medium-high heat until mixture thickens and begins to bubble.
8. Add lemon juice and boil 1 minute, stirring constantly.
9. Fold in drained berries immediately, and fill jars with mixture without delay, leaving 1-inch headspace.
10. Adjust lids, and process immediately following canning directions on page 236.
11. Processing times for pints or quarts are 30 minutes for 1 to 1,000 feet, 35 minutes for 1,001 to 3,000

12. feet, 40 minutes for 3,001 to 6,000 feet, and 45 minutes above 6,000 feet.
13. After processing is complete, turn off heat and remove canner lid.
14. Wait 5 minutes before removing jars.

Yields: 1 quart.

Freezing Blueberries

Make sure you use only ripe, full-flavored blueberries to freeze for the best results.

Ingredients:

blueberries

Directions for whole berries:

1. Sort blueberries; wash quickly in cool water only if very dirty, otherwise freeze as is.
2. Pat dry with paper towels so they will not stick together when freezing.
3. Spread berries in single layer on metal tray; freeze until solid.
4. When frozen, pack in containers and label.
5. When ready to use, simply rinse in running water.
6. To freeze with syrup, pack in containers and cover with 40 percent syrup (3 cups sugar to 4 cups water).

Directions for purée:

1. Wash berries and purée in blender or food processor.
2. Mix 1 cup sugar into each quart of puréed berries.
3. Stir until sugar is dissolved.
4. Pack into containers, leaving 1 inch of headspace.

Triple-Berry Vinegar

This flavorful vinegar is great to have on hand to use in salad dressings.

Ingredients:

- ¼ c. fresh blueberries
- ¼ c. fresh raspberries
- ¼ c. frozen cranberries, thawed
- 8 sage leaves
- 1 c. white wine vinegar
- 3 whole cloves
- 2 cinnamon sticks (3-in. lengths)
- 1 Tbs. sugar
- 8 black peppercorns
- 5 fresh blueberries
- 5 fresh raspberries
- 5 frozen cranberries
- 4 sage leaves

Directions:

1. Combine first 4 ingredients in nonreactive bowl; crush with spoon.
2. Place berry mixture, vinegar, cloves, and cinnamon in wide-mouth jar; cover and let stand 2 weeks in cool, dark place, gently shaking jar occasionally.
3. Strain vinegar mixture through sieve lined with cheesecloth into glass measure or medium bowl, and discard solids.
4. Pour strained vinegar into small nonreactive saucepan, and add sugar.
5. Cook 5 minutes over low heat or until sugar dissolves; cool.
6. Pour into decorative bottle; add peppercorns and remaining ingredients.
7. Seal with cork or other airtight lid.

Yields: 16 servings.

Tri-Berry Jam

Blueberries, raspberries, and strawberries make a colorful, flavorful jam.

Ingredients:

> 4   c. blueberries, fresh or frozen
> 2½ c. red raspberries, fresh or frozen
> 2½ c. strawberries, fresh or frozen
> ¼   c. lemon juice
> 2   pkg. powdered fruit pectin (1¾ oz. each)
> 11 c. sugar

Directions:

1. Combine berries and lemon juice in large kettle; crush fruit slightly.
2. Stir in pectin.
3. Bring to full rolling boil over high heat, stirring constantly.
4. Stir in sugar; return to full rolling boil.
5. Boil 1 minute, stirring constantly.
6. Remove from heat; skim off any foam.
7. Pour hot jam into hot jars, leaving ¼-inch headspace.
8. Adjust caps and process for 15 minutes in boiling-water bath, following canning directions on page 186.

Yields: About 6 pints.

Did You Know?....

Did you know that beginning around 2003, pure or blended blueberry juice became a popular product in Canada and the United States?

Blueberry Juice

This is a great way to preserve some of your blueberries so you have it available year round to use in recipes calling for juice.

Ingredients:

blueberries

Directions:

1. Sort and wash berries.
2. Place in large cooking pot, and cover with water.
3. Cook just below boiling point for 30 minutes.
4. Strain through double thickness of cheesecloth; discard pulp.
5. Can as is or add 1 cup sugar to each gallon of juice for a smooth drink.
6. Pour hot juice into canning jars, and process following canning directions on page 236.

Blueberry Chutney

Chutneys are great over poultry or main entrées. This chutney is very colorful and full of flavor.

Ingredients:

4   c. blueberries, frozen or fresh
1   can whole-berry cranberry sauce (16 oz.)
¼   c. sugar
3   Tbs. balsamic vinegar
1½ tsp. grated orange peel
1   tsp. ground ginger
¼   tsp. crushed red pepper or to taste
¼   tsp. ground black pepper

Directions:

1. In medium nonreactive saucepan, combine all ingredients.
2. Bring to a boil; boil uncovered, stirring frequently, until slightly thickened, 15 to 20 minutes.
3. Pour into clean jars; cover and refrigerate up to 3 weeks.
4. You may also place in canning jars and process following canning directions on page 236, or place in covered plastic containers and freeze.

Yields: 3 cups.

Dried Blueberries

Here is a good way to keep those blueberries you worked so hard to pick. It is nice to enjoy them all year round, and this is a convenient way to store them.

Ingredients:

blueberries, rinsed
lemon juice

Directions:

1. Rinse blueberries and let sit in lemon juice for 1 hour.
2. Make small cut or hole in each berry; spread out to dry on paper towels and wire rack about 2 to 3 days or until roughly consistency of raisins.
3. May also dry in food dehydrator using manufacturer's instructions, on a screen in a gas oven with only the pilot light on, or hang them with a needle and thread.
4. Store in airtight container for up to 1 month.

Frozen Blueberry Pie Filling

Freezing your pie filling makes it quick and easy to make pies at a later date.

Ingredients:

    12 c. blueberries
    3 c. sugar
    ¾ c. cornstarch
    1 Tbs. grated lemon peel
    ¼ c. lemon juice

Directions:

1. Wash and drain blueberries.
2. Combine sugar and cornstarch in saucepan.
3. Stir blueberries into sugar mixture, and let stand until juice begins to flow from berries, about 30 minutes.
4. Add lemon peel and juice.
5. Cook over medium heat until mixture begins to thicken.
6. Ladle filling into freezer containers or bags, leaving ½-inch headspace.
7. Cool to room temperature for 2 hours before freezing.

Yields: 5 pints.

Did You Know? . . . .

Did you know that highbush blueberries were first introduced to Germany and the Netherlands in the 1930s and have since spread to Poland and Italy, as well as other countries of Europe?

Blueberry Pemmican

This version uses peanut butter rather than melted suet or lard as the binding agent, which is more palatable for today's health-conscious diets.

Ingredients:

    1 c. jerky, beef or venison
    1 c. dried blueberries (recipe page 253)
    1 c. unroasted sunflower seeds (or any crushed nuts)
    2 tsp. honey
    ¼ c. peanut butter
    ½ tsp. cayenne (optional)

Directions:

1. Grind or pound dried meat to mealy powder.
2. Add dried berries and seeds or nuts.
3. Heat honey, peanut butter, and cayenne until softened.
4. Blend all ingredients.
5. When cooled, store in plastic bag or sausage casing in cool, dry place. (It will keep for months.)

Yields: 3 cups.

Did You Know? . . . .

Did you know that Quebec has the largest quantity of wild blueberry production, coming especially from the regions of Saguenay-Lac-Saint-Jean and Côte-Nord, which provide 40 percent of Quebec's total provincial production?

Pickled Blueberries

Try this unique treat!

Ingredients:

    1½ tsp. mixed pickling spice
    1¾ c. sugar
    1½ c. cider vinegar
    ¾   c. water
    1   cinnamon stick
    2   pt. blueberries, washed, picked over

Directions:

1. Tie pickling spice in double-thickness cheesecloth bag.
2. Stir together spice bag, sugar, vinegar, water, and cinnamon stick in large nonreactive saucepan.
3. Simmer uncovered for 20 minutes.
4. Add blueberries; simmer 3 minutes or just until berries become softened.
5. Pour mixture into large bowl; cover and refrigerate overnight.
6. Remove spice bag and cinnamon stick, and use slotted spoon to serve.
7. If not using immediately, spoon into sterilized canning jars; refrigerate.

Did You Know? . . . .

Did you know that blueberries belong to the Ericaceae *family of plants, which includes cranberry, azalea, rhododendron, and heather plants?*

Blueberry Delights Cookbook

A Collection of Blueberry Recipes
Cookbook Delights Series-Book 2

Salads

Table of Contents

Did You Know? . . . .

Did you know that although they are called "blue" berries, blueberries grow in a variety of shades from light blue to dark purple?

Wild Rice Blueberry Salad

This salad is easy to make and tastes wonderful. Wild rice is much healthier than white rice, and the taste is delicious!

Ingredients:

1 pkg. wild rice (6 oz.)
¾ c. light mayonnaise
1 tsp. white vinegar
1 tsp. sugar
1 c. dried blueberries (recipe page 253)
¼ c. diced green onion
1 c. seedless red grapes
8 oz. blanched slivered almonds
salt and pepper to taste

Directions:

1. Cook rice according to package directions.
2. Remove from heat and set aside to cool.
3. In medium bowl whisk together mayonnaise, vinegar, sugar, salt, and pepper.
4. Stir in rice, dried blueberries, onion, and grapes until evenly coated with dressing.
5. Cover and refrigerate for 1 to 2 hours.
6. Before serving, sprinkle top of salad with slivered almonds.

Did You Know? . . . .

Did you know that to benefit from all of the anthocyanin in the pigments in blueberries, during cooking you should make sure to integrate the skins of the blueberry?

Sugar Snap Pea and Berry Salad

This is a delicious summer salad that combines the crispness of snap peas with healthy salad greens and berries.

Ingredients:

    ½ lb. sugar snap peas, trimmed
    1 c. fresh raspberries, divided
    2 Tbs. raspberry vinegar
    2 Tbs. olive oil
    1 pinch sugar
    1 c. fresh blueberries
    2 c. torn mixed salad greens
    salt and pepper to taste

Directions:

1. Bring pot of water to a boil; place snap peas in pot, and cook 1 to 2 minutes.
2. Drain, rinse under cold water, and set aside.
3. Place about 1½ tablespoon raspberries in strainer over bowl, and crush with wooden spoon; discard pulp.
4. Mix vinegar, olive oil, sugar, salt, and pepper with strained raspberry juice.
5. In large bowl gently toss dressing with snap peas, remaining raspberries, and blueberries.
6. Cover, and chill at least 30 minutes in refrigerator.
7. Toss with greens just before serving.

Yields: 6 servings.

Did You Know? . . . .

Did you know that August is Blueberry Month in British Columbia?

Chicken Pasta Salad with Blueberries

This salad makes a tasty and healthy lunch or light supper.

Ingredients:

- 3   c. spiral pasta
- 1   c. pea pods, trimmed, cut in half
- 2   c. cooked chicken (about 1 lb.), cubed
- 1   c. sliced celery
- 1   c. fresh blueberries
- ½   c. finely chopped red pepper
- ¼   c. chopped parsley
- ¼   c. chopped red onion
- 1¼ c. red wine vinegar dressing, divided
- 2-3 Tbs. chopped fresh basil
- ½   c. freshly grated Parmesan cheese
-       salt and pepper to taste

Directions:

1. Cook pasta according to directions on package.
2. About 1 minute before it is finished, add pea pods, then drain and rinse with cold water.
3. In large bowl mix pasta and pea pods along with chicken, celery, blueberries, red pepper, parsley, onion, ¼ cup red wine vinegar dressing, basil, salt, and pepper.
4. Toss with ½ cup red wine vinegar dressing.
5. Cover; refrigerate several hours or overnight to blend flavors.
6. Before serving, toss with remaining ½ cup dressing and Parmesan cheese.

Yields: 12 servings (1 cup each).

Dried Blueberry Chicken Salad

When fresh blueberries are out of season, you can make this chicken salad with dried berries.

Ingredients:

    4 c. cooked chicken, 1-inch dice
    1 c. dried blueberries (recipe page 253)
    ½ c. slivered almonds, toasted
    ½ c. mayonnaise
    ¼ c. dairy sour cream
    1 Tbs. lemon juice
    ¼ c. chutney
    ½ tsp. salt
    ⅛ tsp. pepper
    lettuce leaves

Directions:

1. Combine chicken, dried blueberries, and almonds.
2. In separate bowl combine mayonnaise, sour cream, lemon juice, chutney, salt, and pepper; add to chicken mixture and toss well.
3. Cover and chill.
4. Serve on lettuce leaves.

Yields: 6 servings.

Did You Know? . . . .

Did you know that in the past, blueberries were used for medicinal purposes along with the leaves and root? They were used to treat cough and were said to be good for the blood.

Carrot Salad with Wild Blueberries

This salad is full of good-for-you ingredients, and it is delicious.

Ingredients:

- 4 tsp. maple syrup
- ½ tsp. salt
- 1 c. diced red pepper
- 2 tsp. olive oil
- 1½ c. frozen wild blueberries
- 1 bunch carrots or 10-oz. bag of matchstick carrots
- ⅓ c. roasted walnuts
- ½ c. pineapple pieces
- juice of 1 lemon

Directions:

1. Mix lemon juice with maple syrup, salt, red pepper, and olive oil.
2. Add blueberries and let them defrost in marinade.
3. Peel carrots and cut into very thin slices (or use prepared matchstick carrots).
4. Make 8 carrot ribbons with potato peeler for garnish.
5. Chop walnuts and roast in coated pan.
6. Cut pineapple into small cubes.
7. Mix carrots, walnuts, and pineapple pieces, then carefully mix into marinated blueberries.
8. Serve soon after mixing in berries.

Yields: 6 servings.

Did You Know? . . . .

Did you know that over 20 varieties of blueberries are grown in Michigan?

Blueberry Salsa Salad

This is a deliciously different salad. It is a mix of several different flavors and textures.

Ingredients:

- 2 c. fresh blueberries
- 1 med. red apple, diced
- 1 lg. navel orange, peeled, sectioned, chopped
- ½ c. finely chopped sweet onion
- 1-2 Tbs. minced fresh cilantro
- ¼ c. red wine vinegar
- 3 Tbs. unsweetened apple juice
- 2 Tbs. sugar
- 2 Tbs. olive oil
- ¼ tsp. salt
- 1 pkg. spring mix salad greens (5 oz.)
- ½ c. crumbled blue cheese

Directions:

1. In large bowl combine blueberries, apple, orange, onion, and cilantro.
2. In small bowl whisk together vinegar, apple juice, sugar, oil, and salt.
3. Drizzle over fruit mixture and toss to coat; let stand for 10 minutes.
4. Divide salad greens among 6 serving plates.
5. Using slotted spoon, arrange blueberry salsa over greens.
6. Drizzle with dressing left in bowl, then sprinkle with blue cheese.

Yields: 6 servings.

Wild Blueberries with Roquefort and Celery

Depending on how you cut up the celery, this recipe can be used as a salad or as an appetizer.

Ingredients for salad:

> 2 c. frozen wild blueberries
> ½ c. walnuts
> ½ c. Roquefort or blue cheese, crumbled
> 1 bunch celery
> 6 Tbs. Cumberland sauce (recipe below)

Ingredients for Cumberland sauce:

> ⅓ c. ruby port
> 1 tsp. currant jelly (or other fruit jelly)
> 1 pinch cayenne
> juice and zest of ½ orange and ½ lemon

Directions for salad:

1. Let blueberries defrost.
2. Chop walnuts into small pieces, and roast gently in coated pan without fat.
3. Divide Roquefort into bits.
4. Clean and wash celery; cut into ½-inch pieces.
5. Toss lightly with cheese, walnuts, and blueberries.
6. Drizzle with Cumberland sauce, and serve on a leaf of Boston lettuce.
7. Alternatively, cut celery into 3-inch pieces.
8. Fill celery pieces with combined mixture of blueberries, walnuts, and cheese.
9. Drizzle each filled celery piece with Cumberland sauce.

Directions for Cumberland sauce:

1. Combine all ingredients, and simmer until reduced by ½ or until thickened enough to coat a spoon.

Yields: 6 servings.

Berry Nectarine Salad

The contrast in colors between the nectarines, raspberries, and blueberries makes this a pretty as well as a tasty salad.

Ingredients:

4 med. nectarines, unpeeled, sliced
¼ c. sugar
½ tsp. ground ginger
1 tsp. lemon juice
2 c. fresh raspberries
1 c. fresh blueberries
3 oz. cream cheese, softened

Directions:

1. Place nectarines in large bowl.
2. Combine sugar and ginger; sprinkle over nectarines and gently stir to evenly coat.
3. Drizzle with lemon juice; cover and refrigerate for 1 hour, stirring once.
4. Drain and reserve liquid.
5. Gently stir raspberries and blueberries into nectarines.
6. In small mixing bowl beat cream cheese until smooth.
7. Gradually beat in reserved liquid, then spoon over fruit and serve immediately.

Yields: 8 servings.

Blueberry Banana Salad

This delicious fruit salad is a great dish to serve at a holiday meal or take to a potluck.

Ingredients:

    2   c. sliced firm bananas
    1½ c. fresh blueberries
    1   can Mandarin oranges (11 oz.), drained
    ½   c. miniature marshmallows
    2   Tbs. flaked coconut
    ½   c. sour cream

Directions:

1. In large bowl combine bananas, blueberries, oranges, marshmallows, and coconut.
2. Gently fold in sour cream.
3. Refrigerate leftovers.

Yields: 6 servings.

Blueberry Potato Salad

Blueberries add color and texture to this potato salad.

Ingredients:

    ¼ c. white wine vinegar
    1 Tbs. olive oil
    ½ tsp. sugar
    ½ tsp. salt
    ½ tsp. dried basil, crushed
    ⅛ tsp. black pepper
    4 lg. red potatoes, cooked, sliced
    1 c. fresh blueberries
    ½ c. diced cucumber

½ c. shredded carrot

2 Tbs. chopped scallions

2 Tbs. chopped fresh parsley

Directions:

1. Prepare dressing by combining vinegar, oil, sugar, salt, basil, and pepper; blend well.
2. In large bowl combine dressing with potatoes, mixing well.
3. Stir in blueberries, cucumber, and carrot.
4. Sprinkle with chopped scallions and parsley.

Blueberry Spinach Salad

This tasty salad is destined to become a favorite.

Ingredients:

½ c. vegetable oil

¼ c. raspberry vinegar

2 tsp. Dijon mustard

1 tsp. sugar

½ tsp. salt

⅛ tsp. freshly ground pepper

1 pkg. fresh spinach (10 oz.), torn

1 pkg. blue cheese (4 oz.), crumbled

1 c. fresh blueberries

½ c. chopped pecans, toasted

Directions:

1. In jar with tight-fitting lid, combine oil, vinegar, mustard, salt, and pepper; shake well.
2. In large salad bowl, toss spinach, blue cheese, blueberries, and pecans.
3. Add dressing and toss gently; serve immediately.

Yields: 6 to 8 servings.

Mixed Fruit Salad

This colorful salad is a medley of fruits. The apples add crunch and the lemon sauce is refreshing.

Ingredients:

    1 lg. green apple, chopped
    1 med. red apple, chopped
    ½ c. seedless red grapes, halved
    ½ c. green grapes, halved
    1 can unsweetened pineapple tidbits (8 oz.), drained
    ½ c. blueberries, fresh or frozen
    ¾ c. Mandarin oranges, drained
    ¼ c. sugar
    ¼ c. lemon juice
    ¼ c. water

Directions:

1. In serving bowl combine apples, grapes, pineapple, blueberries, and oranges.
2. In small bowl combine sugar, lemon juice, and water; stir until sugar is dissolved.
3. Pour over fruit and toss gently.
4. Serve with slotted spoon.

Yields: 6 servings.

Did You Know? . . . .

Did you know that the blue paint used to paint woodwork in Shaker houses was made from sage blossoms, indigo, and blueberry skins, mixed in milk?

Blueberry Coleslaw

This is a fruity, refreshing twist on coleslaw.

Ingredients:

- 1 med. head green cabbage, shredded
- 1 sm. red onion, minced
- ½ c. chopped parsley
- 2 Tbs. minced orange zest
- 1 c. mayonnaise
- ½ c. sour cream
- ¼ c. blueberry vinegar (recipe page 188)
- 3 Tbs. freshly squeezed orange juice
- ¼ c. sugar
- 1 tsp. ground cloves
- 1 pt. fresh blueberries
- salt
- freshly ground black pepper
- orange slices for garnish

Directions:

1. In large bowl toss together cabbage, onion, parsley, and orange zest.
2. In small bowl whisk together mayonnaise, sour cream, vinegar, orange juice, sugar, and cloves.
3. Taste, then season with salt and pepper.
4. Pour dressing over cabbage mixture, and toss until well coated.
5. Toss with blueberries, garnish with orange slices, and serve.

Did You Know? . . . .

Did you know that Blueberry Jelly Bellies were created especially for Ronald Reagan?

Blueberry and Tortellini Fruit Salad

Three-cheese tortellini pasta is found in the refrigerated section of your grocery store. You may use various other fruits such as bananas, peaches, apples, and oranges in this salad for a change of pace.

Ingredients:

 1 pkg. three-cheese tortellini pasta (9 oz.)
 1 c. fresh blueberries
 1 c. sliced fresh strawberries
 1 can Mandarin orange segments (11 oz.), drained
 ¾ c. green grapes
 ¼ c. sliced almonds
 ½ c. poppy seed dressing

Directions:

1. Cook pasta according to directions on package; drain.
2. In large bowl mix pasta and salad ingredients.
3. Pour dressing over salad and toss lightly.
4. Refrigerate until ready to serve.

Yields: 6 servings (1 cup each).

Did You Know? . . . .

Did you know that British Columbia is the second largest producer of cultivated blueberries in the world, following Michigan?

Side Dishes

Table of Contents

Did You Know? . . . .

Did you know that blueberries may change color when cooked? Acids, such as lemon juice and vinegar, cause the blue pigment in the berries to turn reddish.

Blueberry Rice Salad

This tasty side dish goes great with lamb kabobs.

Ingredients:
- 3 c. cooked rice, room temperature
- ½ c. toasted sliced almonds
- 1 c. fresh blueberries
- ½ c. vinaigrette

Directions:
1. To toast sliced almonds, preheat oven to 350 degrees F.
2. Place sliced almonds in single layer on jellyroll pan or baking sheet.
3. Place in middle of oven for approximately 5 minutes or until lightly toasted. (Watch carefully because they burn easily.)
4. In medium bowl combine rice, blueberries, and almonds; lightly toss to combine.
5. Stir vinaigrette and measure ½ cup; add to rice mixture and lightly toss.
6. Taste; add a little more vinaigrette if necessary.

Blueberry Corn Salad

Berries have so many health benefits. This colorful side dish is another great way of adding more of them to your diet.

Ingredients:
- 1 c. frozen whole kernel corn
- ¼ c. chopped onions
- ¼ c. white vinegar
- 2 tablespoons honey

1 serrano pepper, finely chopped

⅛ tsp. salt

¼ tsp. ground cardamom

½ c. chopped jicama

1 c. fresh blueberries, rinsed, drained

Directions:

1. In medium saucepan combine corn kernels, onion, vinegar, honey, and chopped pepper.
2. Stir in salt and cardamom, and bring mixture to a boil; reduce heat and cook, uncovered, over medium heat for 4 minutes or until corn is tender.
3. Remove from heat, cool slightly, and stir in jicama.
4. Cover and chill at least 2 hours
5. Just before serving, gently stir in rinsed blueberries.

Warm Wild Rice with Blueberries

Wild and brown rice, avocados, sunflower seeds, and blueberries make this a flavorful and healthy side dish.

Ingredients:

3 c. cooked wild and brown rice, cooled

2 avocados, cut into bite-size pieces

1 c. diced fresh fennel bulb or 2 Tbs. fennel seeds

1 c. diced celery

½ pkg. dried blueberries

¼ c. sunflower seeds

¼ c. raisins

¼ c. chopped fresh dill

Directions:

1. Combine all ingredients in bowl.
2. Serve at room temperature.

Blueberry Polenta

This will taste quite rich, and the warm blueberries are an extra flavor treat.

Ingredients:

2	whole bananas, very ripe
1	c. corn flour
½	c. whole-wheat flour
2	Tbs. honey
1	Tbs. sugar
½	c. water or nonfat milk
1	egg white
¼	tsp. guar gum or other thickener
½	tsp. baking soda
2	Tbs. yogurt
½	tsp. ground cinnamon
½	tsp. ground cardamom
1½	c. fresh blueberries

Directions:

1. Preheat oven to 400 degrees F.
2. Mash bananas with potato masher.
3. Add all remaining ingredients except for blueberries; stir well.
4. Lightly oil small pan (8 x 5 inches) or 8-muffin tin, or spray with cooking spray.
5. Pour batter into pan or muffin tin.
6. Sprinkle top with blueberries, the more the better. (Blueberries will not sink to bottom, so press them down if you want to get even more of them in.)
7. Bake about 25 to 35 minutes.
8. Serve warm.

Yields: 12 servings.

Blintz Soufflé with Blueberries

Here is a soufflé that will complement the wonderful taste of any main dish you want to put on the table!

Ingredients:

- 8 oz. cream cheese, softened
- 2 c. small curd cottage cheese
- 2 egg yolks
- ⅓ c. plus 1 Tbs. sugar, divided
- 1 tsp. vanilla extract
- 6 whole eggs
- 1½ c. sour cream
- ½ c. orange juice
- ½ c. butter, softened
- 1 c. all-purpose flour
- 2 tsp. baking powder
- 1 tsp. grated orange rind
- 1½ c. fresh blueberries

Directions:

1. Preheat oven to 350 degrees F.
2. In large bowl cream together cream cheese, cottage cheese, egg yolks, 1 tablespoon sugar, and vanilla; blend well.
3. In separate bowl beat together whole eggs, sour cream, orange juice, and butter.
4. Sift together flour, remaining ⅓ cup sugar, and baking powder; add to above egg and juice ingredients; stir in orange rind and blend until smooth.
5. Pour half of batter into greased 13 x 9 x 2-inch baking pan; spoon cream cheese mixture over batter, and smooth with knife.
6. Pour remaining batter on top of cream cheese layer; sprinkle blueberries over top.
7. Bake for 50 to 60 minutes, until puffy and golden.
8. Remove from oven and serve immediately.

Blueberry Alla Checca

Here is a wonderful recipe for an uncooked sauce made with fresh blueberries and garden tomatoes. You do not have to cook a thing except for the pasta! What a delicious side dish this makes to complement your meal.

Ingredients:

    1½ c. fresh blueberries
    5   med. tomatoes, seeded, diced, drained
    4   cloves garlic, minced
    ½   c. chopped fresh basil
    ½   c. olive oil
    ½   c. red wine
    1   lb. pasta
       grated Parmesan cheese

Directions:

1. Combine blueberries, tomatoes, garlic, basil, olive oil, and wine in nonmetal bowl.
2. Cover with plastic wrap; allow sitting at room temperature at least 2 hours or as long as 10 hours to marinate flavors.
3. Cook pasta in large pot of boiling salted water until al dente; drain well.
4. Pour uncooked sauce over hot pasta; toss.
5. Serve with grated Parmesan cheese on the side.

Yields: 4 servings.

Did You Know? . . . .

Did you know that the lowbush blueberry, a native plant, is also grown commercially in Canada and Maine, mainly harvested from managed wild patches?

Blueberry Fresh Fruit Cocktail

Adding blueberries gives a new twist to fruit cocktail. Serve this fruit cocktail as a special chilled side dish or as a sweet treat.

Ingredients:

- 2 c. apple juice
- 1 Tbs. lemon juice
- ½ tsp. lemon or orange zest
- 2 cinnamon sticks (3-in. lengths)
- 1 c. fresh blueberries
- 1 c. fresh pineapple (may use canned if necessary)
- 2 Red Delicious apples, unpeeled, cored, cubed
- 1 orange, peeled, sectioned, halved
- ½ c. sm. seedless grapes or halve large ones
- 1 c. sour cream
- ¼ c. grated coconut
- ¼ c. apricot preserves
- 2 Tbs. dry white wine
- ½ c. chopped macadamia nuts

Directions:

1. In medium saucepan combine apple juice, lemon juice, orange or lemon zest, and cinnamon sticks.
2. Heat to boiling; simmer uncovered for 10 minutes, then cool to room temperature.
3. In large serving bowl combine blueberries, pineapple, apples, orange, and grapes.
4. Remove cinnamon sticks, and pour apple juice mixture over fruit; let marinate for 30 minutes.
5. Combine sour cream, coconut, preserves, wine, and nuts; blend well.
6. Completely drain fruits until no dripping is seen; combine with sour cream mixture.
7. Toss and serve immediately, or chill until ready to serve.

Yields: 6 servings.

Blueberry Onion Wild Rice Stuffing

The mingling of flavors in this stuffing goes well with any fowl.

Ingredients:

 1 lb. breakfast sausage
 ½ onion, diced
 ½ green pepper, diced
 3 c. bread cubes
 ½ c. chicken broth
 1 c. cooked wild rice
 ½ c. dried blueberries (recipe page 253)
 4 slices bacon

Directions:

1. Preheat oven to 350 degrees F.
2. In skillet brown sausage, onion, and green pepper; drain off fat.
3. In large bowl toss together bread cubes and chicken broth until moist.
4. Add sausage, rice, and blueberries, mixing thoroughly.
5. Place in greased casserole dish; lay strips of bacon over top and cover.
6. Bake for 20 minutes; remove cover, and bake an additional 5 minutes or until bacon is browned and starts to crisp.
7. Remove from oven and serve while hot.

Yields: 4 servings.

Did You Know? . . . .

Did you know that 12,000 acres of farmland in British Columbia are devoted to growing blueberries?

Multigrain Blueberry Pilaf

We love wild rice, and the addition of blueberries to this pilaf makes it very tasty and colorful.

Ingredients:

- ¾ c. chopped pecans, toasted
- ⅔ c. wild rice
- ½ c. wheat berries
- 1 c. chopped onion
- 3 cloves garlic, finely chopped
- 2 Tbs. butter
- 1 Tbs. olive oil
- 2½ c. chicken broth
- 2½ tsp. rubbed sage
- ¼ tsp. ground pepper
- ⅓ c. brown rice
- 1½ c. blueberries

Directions:

1. Preheat oven to 350 degrees F.
2. Spread pecans in ungreased pan; bake just until browned; set aside.
3. Rinse wild rice and wheat berries under cold running water; drain well.
4. In large saucepan cook onion and garlic in olive oil and butter over medium heat for about 10 minutes or until tender.
5. Stir in drained wild rice and wheat berries, chicken broth, sage, and pepper.
6. Bring to boiling then reduce heat; cover and simmer for 30 minutes.
7. Stir brown rice into wild rice mixture; return to boiling.
8. Reduce heat; cover and simmer for about 45 minutes or until grains are tender.
9. Stir blueberries and pecans into rice mixture; serve warm.

Yields: 6 to 8 servings.

Blueberry Raisin Dressing

This delicious dressing goes well with any kind of meat.

Ingredients:

- ½ c. chopped onion
- ½ c. chopped celery
- 3 Tbs. butter
- 1 c. blueberries, fresh or frozen
- ½ c. golden raisins
- 4½ c. dry bread crumbs
- ½ tsp. sage
- ½ c. apple juice
  ground black pepper to taste
  vegetable oil

Directions:

1. Preheat oven to 350 degrees F.
2. Place onion, celery, and butter in skillet over medium-high heat.
3. Sauté for 5 minutes or until vegetables are tender.
4. Transfer into large bowl; add blueberries, raisins, bread crumbs, sage, and pepper, stirring well.
5. Add apple juice and toss lightly.
6. If dressing seems too dry, add more apple juice.
7. Turn into large, lightly oiled baking dish; cover and bake for 45 minutes.
8. Remove from oven and serve while hot.

Yields: 6 servings.

Did You Know? . . . .

Did you know that Nova Scotia produces an average annual blueberry harvest of 30 million pounds?

Blueberry Dumplings

These are some great dumplings to serve with stewed chicken, turkey, or boiled pork roast. See how your family loves them!

Ingredients:

- 4   c. blueberries
- 1½ c. water
- 2   c. sugar, divided
- 2   Tbs. butter, softened
- ½   tsp. vanilla extract
- ½   c. milk
- 1½ c. all-purpose flour
- 2   tsp. baking powder

Directions:

1. In large serving skillet over medium heat, bring berries, water, and 1½ cups sugar to a boil; reduce heat to simmer.
2. In large bowl cream remaining sugar and butter together; add vanilla and milk, blending well.
3. Sift flour and baking powder together; gradually stir into milk mixture just until moistened.
4. Drop into simmering blueberry mixture by tablespoonfuls; cover and simmer 20 minutes or until dumplings test done.
5. Remove serving skillet from stove, and place on table to serve.

Yields: 6 servings.

Did You Know? . . . .

Did you know that the blueberry muffin is the official muffin of Minnesota?

Rosemary-Roasted Sweet Potatoes with Blueberries

Crisp, golden baked sweet potatoes, topped with blueberries and garnished with rosemary sprigs, are a tasty treat as well as a treat for the eyes.

Ingredients:

    3 Tbs. extra-virgin olive oil
    2 tsp. kosher salt
    ¼ tsp. black pepper
    2 tsp. very finely minced fresh rosemary
    4 lg. sweet potatoes (about 4½ lb.)
    1 med. white onion
    ½ c. wild blueberries
        fresh rosemary sprigs for garnish

Directions:

1. Preheat oven to 400 degrees F.
2. Stir olive oil, salt, pepper, and minced rosemary together in large bowl.
3. Peel sweet potatoes, cut in half lengthwise, then cut each half into 6 large, chunky pieces; add to bowl and set aside.
4. Peel onion and trim root end but keep it intact.
5. Cut onion in half vertically, then cut each half into about 6 wedges; add to bowl.
6. With rubber spatula mix potatoes and onions with olive oil mixture to coat vegetables well.
7. Transfer mixture to rimmed baking sheet, and bake for 40 minutes.
8. Remove from oven, and with spatula turn potatoes and onions over.
9. Increase oven to 450 degrees F.; return pan to oven, and bake for another 15 minutes or until potatoes are crisp and golden.

10. Sprinkle blueberries over potatoes, and return to oven for 5 minutes more.
11. Transfer to warmed platter, and garnish with sprigs of fresh rosemary.

Yields: 6 servings.

Blueberry Rice Pilaf

Blueberries add color and flavor to this rice pilaf. It makes a great side dish for your favorite entrée.

Ingredients:

¾ c. chopped onion
1¼ c. chopped celery
½ c. blueberries
⅔ c. chopped walnuts
1 Tbs. chopped fresh thyme (or 1 tsp. dried)
1 Tbs. chopped fresh marjoram (or 1 tsp. dried)
½ tsp. ground black pepper
1 Tbs. butter
3 c. cooked rice

Directions:

1. Put onion, celery, and blueberries in nonstick skillet.
2. Add walnuts, thyme, marjoram, pepper, and butter.
3. Cook uncovered over medium heat for 10 minutes or until vegetables are tender, stirring occasionally.
4. Add rice; mix well.
5. Cook 3 to 4 minutes or until thoroughly heated.
6. Serve while hot with your favorite entrée.

Yields: 4 to 6 servings.

Pasta with Fresh Blueberries, Tomatoes, and Corn

This is a wonderful summertime dish with the great taste of blueberries, garden tomatoes, and fresh corn. It is really fast to prepare and tastes delicious.

Ingredients:

    8 oz. pasta
    5 Tbs. olive oil, divided
    2 Tbs. red wine vinegar
    1 tsp. dried basil
    1 c. fresh blueberries
    ½ c. whole corn kernels, cooked
    2 tomatoes, chopped
    ½ c. chopped green onions or scallions
    1 Tbs. grated Parmesan cheese
    2 tsp. chopped fresh basil for garnish
       salt and ground black pepper to taste

Directions:

1. Cook pasta in large pot of boiling water until al dente, and drain completely; toss with 1 tablespoon olive oil then set aside.
2. Meanwhile, in large bowl whisk together remaining olive oil, red wine vinegar, and basil; add salt and pepper to taste.
3. Stir in blueberries, corn, tomatoes, and scallions; let sit for 10 minutes to marinate flavors.
4. To serve, toss with pasta, and sprinkle with grated Parmesan cheese and fresh basil if desired.

Yields: 4 servings.

Blueberry Delights Cookbook
A Collection of Blueberry Recipes
Cookbook Delights Series-Book 2

Soups

Table of Contents

Page

Did You Know?....

Did you know that a blueberry with any hint of red is not fully ripened, and once picked; blueberries will not ripen any further?

Fresh Peach Blueberry Soup

You can vary the fruits in this soup, depending on what is available at the time.

Ingredients:

  3 c. diced honeydew melon
  ½ c. fresh orange juice
  ½ c. vanilla yogurt
  1 Tbs. honey
  1 tsp. finely chopped, peeled gingerroot
  2 tsp. fresh lime juice
  2 c. diced, peeled peaches (1½ lb.)
  1 c. blueberries

Directions:

  1. Place first 6 ingredients in blender, and process until smooth.
  2. Combine melon mixture, diced peaches, and blueberries in bowl; stir well.
  3. Cover and chill before serving.

Yields: 6 servings.

Maine Wild Blueberry Soup

This is a delicious cold soup that is very refreshing on a warm summer day.

Ingredients:

  4½ c. fresh wild blueberries
  1   c. Pinot Noir
  ¼   c. honey
      vanilla crème fraîche for garnish

Directions:

1. In food processor combine blueberries, Pinot Noir, and honey; blend until mixture becomes smooth. (Do not strain.)
2. Chill soup before serving.
3. Garnish each soup bowl with vanilla crème fraîche.

Yields: 4 servings.

Norwegian Blueberry Soup

Make sure to use freshly squeezed orange and lemon juice in this soup for the best flavor.

Ingredients:

1 env. unflavored gelatin
¼ c. cold water
4 c. fresh orange juice
3 Tbs. fresh lemon juice
¼ c. sugar
2 c. fresh blueberries, washed
   fresh mint for garnish

Directions:

1. Soften gelatin in cold water in custard cup.
2. Place in pan of hot (not boiling) water until melted and ready to use.
3. Combine juices and sugar with melted gelatin.
4. Stir until sugar and gelatin are dissolved.
5. Chill until mixture begins to thicken.
6. Fold blueberries into mixture.
7. Chill until ready to serve.
8. Spoon into chilled bouillon cups, and garnish with fresh mint.

Yields: 6 servings.

Mulligan Stew with Blueberry Dumplings

This thick, hearty stew is made unique with the addition of the blueberry dumplings.

Ingredients for stew:

1 chicken (3½-4 lb.), cut in pieces
1 Tbs. unsalted butter
1 Tbs. safflower oil
2 bay leaves
4 fresh thyme sprigs
4 allspice berries
1 med. rutabaga, peeled, cut in ½-in. cubes
1 lg. potato, peeled, cut in 2-in. cubes
4 sm. carrots, peeled, cut in ½-in. cubes
2 c. green peas, fresh or frozen
3 sm. parsnips, cut in ½-in. cubes
 salt and freshly ground pepper

Ingredients for dumplings:

2 c. all-purpose flour
1 Tbs. baking powder
½ tsp. baking soda
1 tsp. salt
¼ tsp. freshly grated nutmeg
1 egg, beaten
3 Tbs. unsalted butter, melted
⅔ c. buttermilk
½ c. coarsely chopped wild blueberries, fresh or frozen

Directions for stew:

1. Rinse chicken well and pat thoroughly dry.
2. Heat butter and oil in large (at least 8-quart), heavy stockpot or Dutch oven over medium-high heat.
3. When hot, add chicken pieces, season generously with salt and pepper, and brown on both sides, seasoning the other side when you turn pieces.

4. Brown chicken in several batches to avoid crowding pan, 8 minutes per batch.
5. Transfer chicken to plate or bowl, drain off half the fat in pan, and then return chicken to pan.
6. Add enough water to just cover chicken, and then add herbs and rutabaga.
7. Cover and, leaving heat at medium-high, bring to a boil.
8. Cook until rutabaga is nearly soft through but still somewhat crisp, about 10 minutes.
9. Add potato and carrots; cover, and cook until carrots are nearly tender, about 15 minutes.
10. Adjust seasoning of stew; make sure it is boiling merrily, then stir in peas and parsnips.

Directions for dumplings:

1. While stew is cooking, make dumpling dough.
2. Sift flour, baking powder, baking soda, salt, and nutmeg together into medium bowl.
3. Make well in middle and add egg, melted butter, and buttermilk; mix together in well with small whisk, a fork, or your fingers.
4. Working quickly, incorporates dry ingredients to make fairly stiff dough.
5. Fold in blueberries.
6. One heaping tablespoon at a time, drop dumpling dough on top of stew so dumplings are not touching.
7. Cover, and cook just until dumplings are puffed and cooked through, no longer than 15 minutes.
8. Check them occasionally to be sure they do not overcook and become dry.
9. To serve, cut through dumplings with serving spoon, and ladle chicken and vegetables into warmed shallow soup bowls (remove thyme and bay leaves).
10. Place dumplings on top; serve immediately.

Yields: 8 servings.

Blueberry Banana Soup

This chilled soup is a combination of blueberries, apple juice, and bananas.

Ingredients:

- 4 bananas
- 3 Tbs. lemon juice
- 6 c. apple juice, divided
- ¼ c. sugar
- 1½ Tbs. cornstarch
- ½ tsp. ground cinnamon
- 2½ c. heavy cream
- 2 c. blueberries

Directions:

1. In processor, purée bananas with lemon juice.
2. Place in pot, and bring to a boil with 3½ cups apple juice.
3. Blend cornstarch with remaining apple juice; add to soup.
4. Simmer 2 minutes, then remove from heat and chill.
5. Add cinnamon to cream, and then whip into soup.
6. Stir in berries.
7. Serve in chilled soup bowls.

Did You Know? . . . .

Did you know that lowbush species are fire-tolerant, and blueberry production often increases following a forest fire because the plants regenerate rapidly and benefit from removal of competing vegetation?

Blueberry Raspberry Swirl Soup

This soup is a delightful combination of blueberries and raspberries. The swirled effect makes a very nice presentation.

Ingredients:

  1¼ c. fresh blueberries, divided
  1   pkg. unsweetened frozen raspberries (10 oz.), thawed
  ½ c. buttermilk
  ½ c. plain yogurt
  ½ c. vanilla-flavored yogurt

Directions:

1. Place 1 cup blueberries in blender or food processor, and process until very smooth.
2. Pour through strainer to remove skins.
3. To strained blueberries add buttermilk and plain yogurt, stirring to mix well.
4. Refrigerate until thoroughly chilled.
5. Place raspberries in strainer, and with back of a spoon, press berries to remove juice and pulp, discarding seeds.
6. Stir vanilla yogurt into raspberries.
7. Refrigerate until thoroughly chilled.
8. To serve soup, divide blueberry mixture between two bowls.
9. Divide raspberry mixture in half, and carefully add to one side of blueberry mixture in each bowl.
10. With tip of a knife, swirl blueberry and raspberry mixtures together.
11. Garnish soup with remaining ¼ cup blueberries.

Yields: 2 servings.

Peach Cantaloupe Soup with Blueberries

There is nothing in this delicious soup but fruit and a bit of nutmeg!

Ingredients:

> 6 fresh peaches, peeled, sliced
> 1 c. orange juice
> ½ tsp. ground nutmeg
> ½ lg. cantaloupe
>   blueberries

Directions:

1. Simmer peach slices in orange juice with nutmeg. (Cinnamon may be substituted for the nutmeg if desired.)
2. Purée peaches, adding cantaloupe until all is puréed; taste resulting 'soup.'
3. Thin with orange juice if too thick, and add a touch of honey or sugar if not sweet enough for your taste.
4. Chill.
5. Serve garnished with handfuls of fresh blueberries.

Berry Buttermilk Soup

Strawberries may be substituted for the blueberries in this soup.

Ingredients:

> 2 c. blueberries, fresh or frozen loose-pack
> 1½ c. water
> ½ c. sugar
> ½ tsp. finely shredded orange peel
> 2 Tbs. orange juice
> 2 c. buttermilk

Directions:

1. Thaw berries, if frozen, and drain; set aside 5 or 6 berries for garnish.
2. In 1½-quart saucepan combine berries, water, sugar, orange peel, and juice.
3. Bring to boiling, then reduce heat; cover and simmer 20 minutes.
4. Cool 30 minutes.
5. Pour into blender container; cover and blend until smooth.
6. Stir in buttermilk.
7. Cover and chill thoroughly.
8. Garnish with reserved berries or thin orange slice.

Yields: 5 to 6 servings.

Cold Blueberry Soup

This version of a chilled blueberry soup has the added flavor of amaretto.

Ingredients:

2 pt. blueberries, puréed
3 oz. heavy cream
¼ tsp. ground cinnamon
1 tsp. lemon juice
¾ oz. amaretto liqueur

Directions:

1. Mix all ingredients together
2. Serve chilled.

Fruit Soup Plus

If this soup is not sweet enough for your taste, add some canned fruit cocktail, honey, or extra-fine granulated sugar.

Ingredients:

- 8 oz. crushed pineapple
- ½ c. diced strawberries
- ½ pt. fresh blueberries
- 1 c. seedless grape halves
- 1 c. apple juice
- 1 c. orange juice
- 1 c. pineapple juice
- ½ c. vanilla yogurt (optional)

Directions:

1. In large bowl combine pineapple, strawberries, blueberries, and grapes.
2. Pour juices over fruit and stir well.
3. Pour soup into serving bowls or glasses, and garnish each with a dollop of yogurt just before serving.

Yields: 4 servings.

Did You Know? . . . .

Did you know that one obvious difference between blueberries and huckleberries is that the blueberry has many soft, tiny, almost unnoticeable seeds, while the huckleberry has ten larger, hard seeds?

Blueberry Delights Cookbook

A Collection of Blueberry Recipes
Cookbook Delights Series-Book 2

Wines and Spirits

Table of Contents

Page

Did You Know? . . . .

Did you know that North America is the world's leading blueberry producer, currently accounting for nearly 90 percent of world production?

About Cooking with Alcohol

Some recipes in this cookbook contain, among other ingredients, liquors. It is for the purpose of obtaining desired flavor and achieving culinary appreciation and not to be abused in any way. In cooking and baking, alcohol evaporates and only the flavor may be enjoyed. When mixed in cold, however, such as in desserts, caution must be exercised. These recipes are intended for people who may consume small amounts of alcohol in a responsible and safe manner.

I live in Washington State and we are proud of our wine production. Washington State is rapidly gaining prestige as a premier wine producer. Do enjoy the art of wine tasting and enjoy the completeness and uniqueness of each wine. It is an art to enjoy and savor in moderation.

If consumption of even small amounts of alcoholic ingredients presents a problem, in whatever form, please substitute coffee flavor syrups, found in coffee sections of supermarkets. For example, instead of Southern Comfort liqueur, substitute with Irish Cream or Amaretto Syrup.

Karen Jean Matsko Hood

Blueberry Vodka

You can make your own blueberry vodka. It must sit for two weeks, so plan ahead.

Ingredients:
- 1 liter vodka
- 1 pint blueberries, rinsed, dried
- 1 c. raspberry-flavored liqueur

Directions:

1. Pour out approximately ⅓ of the bottle of vodka into holding container; set aside.
2. Score each blueberry with small nick and place into vodka bottle.
3. Using vodka previously set aside, fill vodka bottle until just below neck.
4. Add just enough raspberry liqueurs to top off bottle.
5. Let sit in dark place for 2 weeks.

Yields: 1 liter.

Blueberry Margarita Slush

This icy drink is great at any summer dinner party.

Ingredients:

⅓ c. vodka
2 Tbs. triple sec
⅔ c. blueberries
1 Tbs. lime juice
12 ice cubes
⅔ c. raspberry sorbet

Directions:

1. Combine vodka, triple sec, blueberries, and lime juice in blender; process until blueberries are puréed.
2. Add ice and process until crushed.
3. Blend in raspberry sorbet until slushy.
4. Turn into chilled glasses.

Yields: 4 to 6 servings.

Blue-Woo

This drink is tart and delicious.

Ingredients:

½ oz. vodka
½ oz. blueberry schnapps
   cranberry juice

Directions:

1. Pour vodka and blueberry schnapps in tall glass.
2. Fill with cranberry juice

Yields: 1 serving.

Bluuzberry Shake

This creamy beverage is smooth and tasty.

Ingredients:

4-5 scoops vanilla ice cream
3   oz. blueberry schnapps
3   oz. grape juice
   blueberries for garnish
   strawberry for garnish

Directions:

1. Blend ice cream, schnapps, and juice in blender until thoroughly mixed.
2. Add more ice cream if too thin.
3. Garnish with blueberries and strawberry.

Yields: 1 serving.

Blueberry Eggnog

My family enjoys eggnog, and this makes a colorful drink to enjoy over the holidays or year round.

Ingredients:

- 3 c. whole milk
- 7 lg. eggs
- 1 c. sugar
- 2 c. heavy cream
- 1 tsp. vanilla extract
- ⅓ c. blueberry juice (recipe page 252)
- ⅓ c. Cognac or other brandy (optional)
    freshly grated nutmeg

Directions:

1. Bring milk just to a boil in 2-quart heavy saucepan.
2. Whisk together eggs and sugar in large bowl.
3. Add hot milk in slow stream, whisking.
4. Pour mixture into saucepan, and cook over medium-low heat, stirring constantly with wooden spoon until mixture registers 170 degrees F. on thermometer, 6 to 7 minutes.
5. Pour custard through fine-mesh sieve into clean large bowl, and stir in cream and vanilla.
6. Add blueberry juice and brandy.
7. Cool completely, uncovered, then chill, covered, until cold, at least 3 hours and up to 24 hours.
8. Serve sprinkled with freshly grated nutmeg.
9. Note: Flavor of eggnog improves when made a day ahead to allow alcohol to mellow.

Yields: About 6 cups.

Blueberry Wine

It can be an entertaining project to make your own homemade wine and watch the fermentation process. Make sure all the items are totally clean and sanitized. You may need to order yeast and Campden tablets from a mail order catalog or website if you cannot find them in a local store.

Ingredients:

4 lb. blueberries
2½ lb. sugar
1½ tsp. acid blend
1 tsp. yeast nutrient
1 Campden tablet, crushed
7¼ pt. water
1 pkg. champagne wine yeast

Directions:

1. Put water on to boil.
2. Meanwhile, sort and wash berries, discarding any not sound or ripe.
3. Put blueberries in primary, and mash with sanitized potato masher or piece of hardwood.
4. Add sugar to primary, and pour boiling water over berries and sugar, stirring to dissolve.
5. Cover with sanitized cloth, and set aside to cool to room temperature.
6. When cool, add remaining ingredients except yeast.
7. Stir, cover primary, and set aside for 24 hours.
8. Add activated yeast.
9. When fermentation is vigorous, stir twice daily for 10 days.
10. Strain through nylon straining bag without squeezing.
11. Drip drain 30 to 45 minutes, then pour juice into secondary.
12. Attach airlock and set aside.
13. Rack every 60 days for 6 months, topping up and refitting airlock each time.
14. At last racking, rack into bottles or stabilize, sweeten to taste, wait 10 days, and rack into bottles.

Blueberry Liqueur

This recipe makes a hearty, thick liqueur. Note that it needs to steep for three months and age for at least one month, so you will need to be patient.

Ingredients for liqueur:

    16 oz. frozen blueberries
    1½ c. vodka
    ½ peel of lemon, sliced, scraped
    ¾ c. sugar syrup (recipe below)
    whole cloves

Ingredients for sugar syrup:

    ½ c. sugar
    ¼ c. water

Directions for liqueur:

1. Let blueberries completely thaw.
2. Pour berries and any juice from bag into bowl.
3. Crush with fork and put in 1-liter jar.
4. Peel ½ lemon, scraping pith from back of peel to prevent bitter taste in liqueur. (An apple peeler works best.)
5. Add vodka, lemon peel, and cloves to jar.
6. Steep for 3 months, shaking gently every couple of days to prevent settling.
7. Strain through cheese cloth or jelly bag, squeezing with your hands to get as much liquid as possible; discard solids.
8. Filter liquid through paper towel, coffee filter, or wine/pump filter as many times as needed until it is reasonably free of solids.
9. Add syrup to liqueur, and age for at least 1 month.
10. When bottling, filter again.

Directions for sugar syrup:

1. Bring to a boil together; let stand 1 to 2 minutes before adding to liqueur.

Blue Richie

This is a delicious, fruity beverage with a kick.

Ingredients:

    1½ oz. vanilla vodka
    4   oz. blueberry juice (recipe page 252)
    1   oz. apple juice
    3   fresh blueberries
       ice cubes

Directions:

1. Stir vodka, blueberry juice, and apple juice together in highball glass filled with ice cubes.
2. Top with fresh blueberries.

Yields: 1 serving.

Southern Blues

This drink is perfect for those who want something hard, but do not like the taste.

Ingredients:

    fruit, spice, and whiskey-flavored liqueur
    blueberry schnapps

Directions:

1. Pour liqueur into shot glass, filling ¾ of the way.
2. Top off with blueberry schnapps.

Yields: 1 serving.

Blueberry Freeze

This drink is thick and fruity. It is perfect on a hot summer night.

Ingredients:

- 1 oz. vodka
- ¼ oz. wildberry schnapps
- 1 oz. cream of coconut
- 2 oz. blueberries
- 1½ oz. crushed pineapple
- 1 scoop vanilla ice cream
- 8 oz. crushed ice
- 1 Tbs. whipped cream
  blueberries for garnish

Directions:

1. Blend ingredients thoroughly, and pour into a specialty glass.
2. Top with whipped cream, and garnish with a few blueberries.

Maui Twist

This delicious tropical drink will warm your blood and make you think you are actually in Maui, lounging on the beach.

Ingredients:

- 1 oz. peppermint schnapps
- 1 oz. blackberry brandy
- 2-3 oz. blueberries
- 1 slice lemon
- 2 c. ice

Directions:

1. Blend schnapps, brandy, blueberries, and ice together until smooth, and pour into glasses.
2. Garnish with lemon slice.

Bouncing Baby Blueberry Delight

This is a virgin cocktail that is smooth, rich, and delicious.

Ingredients:

- 1 oz. fresh blueberries
- 1 oz. fresh raspberries
- 1 oz. nonfat plain yogurt
- 1 pineapple ring
- 3 oz. piña colada mix
- crushed ice
- fresh raspberries for garnish
- pineapple wedges for garnish

Directions:

1. Blend all ingredients with crushed ice.
2. Serve in well-chilled tall glass.
3. Garnish with fresh raspberries and pineapple wedges.

Lemon Blueberry Martini

This martini is strong and fruity but not too sweet. A few fresh blueberries finish the presentation.

Ingredients:

- 1 jigger blueberry vodka (recipe page 296)
- 1 jigger vanilla vodka
- 1 jigger Limoncello
- 2 Tbs. fresh blueberries
- ice

Directions:

1. Fill cocktail shaker with ice; pour in blueberry vodka, vanilla vodka, and Limoncello.
2. Cover and shake until outside of shaker is frosty.
3. Strain into chilled martini glass, and garnish with fresh blueberries.

Festival Information

Following is a list of just a few of the blueberry festivals throughout the U.S. and Canada each year. You may use the following contact information or contact the local Chamber of Commerce or Visitor's Information Bureau of each town to find out the exact dates for the festival for that community.

National Blueberry Festival
August each year
South Haven, Michigan
www.blueberryfestival.com

Alyeska Blueberry and Mountain Arts Festival
August each year
Girdwood, Alaska
www.discoveranchorage.net
 /641.cfm
907-754-2209

Brigus Blueberry Festival
August each year
Brigus, Newfoundland, Canada
www.brigus.net

Poplarville Blueberry Jubilee
2nd Saturday of June
Poplarville, Mississippi
www.blueberryjubilee.org

Alabama Blueberry Festival
June each year
Brewton, Alabama
www.brewtonchamber.com
251-867-3224

Marshall County Blueberry Festival
September each year
Plymouth, Indiana
www.blueberryfestival.org
888-936-5020

Texas Blueberry Festival
June each year
Nacogdoches, Texas
www.texasblueberryfestival.com
936-560-5533

Machias Maine Blueberry Festival
August each year
Machias, Maine
www.machiasblueberry.com

Whitesbog Blueberry Festival
June each year
Browns Mills, New Jersey
www.whitesbog.org
(609) 893-4646

Nova Scotia Harvest Festival
August/September each year
Festivals are held in various
 communities
www.wildblueberryfest.com

Blueberry Associations and Commissions

Following are some of the associations or commissions available for blueberry growers.

Carolina Blueberry Association
11421 Hwy 701 North
Garland, NC 28441
Phone: 910-588-4220
www.carolinablueberry.com

Florida Blueberry Growers Association
Contact Sheri Brothers at
Phone: 352-481-5558
Email: fbgaweb@aol.com
www.floridablueberry growers.com

Michigan Blueberry Growers Association
MBG Marketing
P.O. Box 322
Grand Junction, MI 49056
Phone: 269-434-6791
Fax: 269-434-6997
www.blueberries.com

North American Blueberry Council
P.O. Box 1036
Folsom, CA 95763.
Email: info@nabcblues.org
www.nabcblues.org

Texas Blueberry Marketing Association
P. O. Box 635107
Nacogdoches, TX 75963
Phone: 936-559-8585
Fax: 936-559-8588
Email: TBMA@sbcglobal.net

US Highbush Blueberry Council
www.blueberry.org

Washington Blueberry Commission
Alan Schreiber
Washington Ag Development, Inc.
2621 Ringold Road
Eltopia, WA 99330
509-266-4348
Email: aschreib@centurytel.net

Wild Blueberry Association of North America
P.O. Box 100
Old Town, Maine 04468
Phone: 207-570-3535
Fax: 207-581-3499
Email: wildblueberries@gwi.net
www.wildblueberries.com

Wisconsin Berry Growers Association
Anna Maenner, Executive Director WBGA,
Email: info@wiberries.org
www.wiberries.org

U.S. and Metric Measurement Charts

Here are some measurement equivalents to help you with exchanges. There was a time when many people thought the entire world would convert to the metric scale. While most of the world has, America still has not. Metric conversions in cooking are vitally important to preparing a tasty recipe. Here are simple conversion tables that should come in handy.

U.S. Measurement Equivalents

a few grains/pinch/dash (dry) = less than ⅛ teaspoon
a dash (liquid) = a few drops
3 teaspoons = 1 tablespoon
½ tablespoon = 1½ teaspoons
1 tablespoon = 3 teaspoons
2 tablespoons = 1 fluid ounce
4 tablespoons = ¼ cup
5⅓ tablespoons = ⅓ cup
8 tablespoons = ½ cup
8 tablespoons = 4 fluid ounces
10⅔ tablespoons = ⅔ cup
12 tablespoons = ¾ cup
16 tablespoons = 1 cup
16 tablespoons = 8 fluid ounces
⅛ cup = 2 tablespoons
¼ cup = 4 tablespoons
¼ cup = 2 fluid ounces
⅓ cup = 5 tablespoons plus 1 teaspoon
½ cup = 8 tablespoons
1 cup = 16 tablespoons
1 cup = 8 fluid ounces
1 cup = ½ pint
2 cups = 1 pint
2 pints = 1 quart
4 quarts (liquid) = 1 gallon
8 quarts (dry) = 1 peck
4 pecks (dry) = 1 bushel
1 kilogram = approximately 2 pounds
1 liter=approximately 4 cups or 1quart

Approximate Metric Equivalents by Volume

U.S.	Metric
¼ cup	= 60 milliliters
½ cup	= 120 milliliters
1 cup	= 230 milliliters
1¼ cups	= 300 milliliters
1½ cups	= 360 milliliters
2 cups	= 460 milliliters
2½ cups	= 600 milliliters
3 cups	= 700 milliliters
4 cups (1 quart)	= .95 liter
1.06 quarts	= 1 liter
4 quarts (1 gallon)	= 3.8 liters

Approximate Metric Equivalents by Weight

U.S.	Metric
¼ ounce	= 7 grams
½ ounce	= 14 grams
1 ounce	= 28 grams
1¼ ounces	= 35 grams
1½ ounces	= 40 grams
2½ ounces	= 70 grams
4 ounces	= 112 grams
5 ounces	= 140 grams
8 ounces	= 228 grams
10 ounces	= 280 grams
15 ounces	= 425 grams
16 ounces (1 pound)	= 454 grams

Glossary

Aerate: A synonym for sift; to pass ingredients through a fine-mesh device to break up large pieces and incorporate air into ingredients to make them lighter.

Al dente: "To the tooth," in Italian. The pasta is cooked just enough to maintain a firm, chewy texture.

Angostura Bitters: A concentrated bitters for food and beverages made of herbs and spices.

Baste: To brush or spoon liquid fat or juices over meat during roasting to add flavor and prevent drying out.

Bias-slice: To slice a food crosswise at a 45-degree angle.

Blanch: To scald, as in vegetables being prepared for freezing; as in almonds so as to remove skins.

Blend: To mix or fold two or more ingredients together to obtain equal distribution throughout the mixture.

Braise: To brown meat in oil or other fat and then cook slowly in liquid. The effect of braising is to tenderize the meat.

Bread: To coat food with crumbs (usually with soft or dry bread crumbs), sometimes seasoned.

Brown: To quickly sauté, broil, or grill either at the beginning or at the end of meal preparation, often to enhance flavor, texture, or eye appeal.

Brush: To use a pastry brush to coat a food such as meat or pastry with melted butter, glaze, or other liquid.

Butterfly: To cut open a food such as pork chops down the center without cutting all the way through, and then spread apart.

Caramelize: To brown sugar over a flame, with or without the addition of some water to aid the process. The temperature range in which sugar caramelizes is approximately 320 to 360 degrees F.

Clarify: To remove impurities from butter or stock by heating the liquid, then straining or skimming it.

Coddle: A cooking method in which foods (such as eggs) are put in separate containers and placed in a pan of simmering water for slow, gentle cooking.

Confit: To slowly cook pieces of meat in their own gently rendered fat.

Core: To remove the inedible center of fruits such as pineapples.

Cream: To beat vegetable shortening, butter, or margarine, with or without sugar, until light and fluffy. This process traps in air bubbles, later used to create height in cookies and cakes.

Crimp: To create a decorative edge on a pie crust. On a double pie crust, this also seals the edges together.

Curd: A custard-like pie or tart filling flavored with juice and zest of citrus fruit, usually lemon, although lime and orange may also be used.

Curdle: To cause semisolid pieces of coagulated protein to develop in food, usually as a result of the addition of an acid substance or the overheating of milk or egg-based sauces.

Custard: A mixture of beaten egg, milk, and possibly other ingredients such as sweet or savory flavorings, which are cooked with gentle heat, often in a water bath or double boiler. As pie filling, the custard is frequently cooked and chilled before being layered into a baked crust.

Deglaze: To add liquid to a pan in which foods have been fried or roasted, in order to dissolve the caramelized juices stuck to the bottom of the pan.

Dot: To sprinkle food with small bits of an ingredient such as butter to allow for even melting.

Dredge: To sprinkle lightly and evenly with sugar or flour. A dredger has holes pierced on the lid to sprinkle evenly.

Drippings: The liquids left in the bottom of a roasting or frying pan after meat is cooked. Drippings are generally used for gravies and sauces.

Drizzle: To pour a liquid such as a sweet glaze or melted butter in a slow, light trickle over food.

Dust: To sprinkle food lightly with spices, sugar, or flour for a light coating.

Egg Wash: A mixture of beaten eggs (yolks, whites, or whole eggs) with either milk or water. Used to coat cookies and other baked goods to give them a shine when baked.

Emulsion: A mixture of liquids, one being a fat or oil and the other being water based so that tiny globules of one are suspended in the other. This may involve the use of stabilizers, such as egg or custard. Emulsions may be temporary or permanent.

Entrée: A French term that originally referred to the first course of a meal, served after the soup and before the meat courses. In the United States, it refers to the main dish of a meal.

Fillet: To remove the bones from meat or fish for cooking.

Filter: To remove lumps, excess liquid, or impurities by passing through paper or cheesecloth.

Firm-Ball Stage: In candy making, the point at which boiling syrup dropped in cold water forms a ball that is compact yet gives slightly to the touch.

Flambé: To ignite a sauce or other liquid so that it flames.

Flan: An open pie filled with sweet or savory ingredients; also, a Spanish dessert of baked custard covered with caramel.

Flute: To create a decorative scalloped or undulating edge on a pie crust or other pastry.

Framboise: A brandy or liqueur made from raspberries.

Frizzle: To cook thin slices of meat in hot oil until crisp and slightly curly.

Fromage Blanc: A dairy product originating from Belgium and the north of France. It literally means "white cheese." Fromage blanc is unlike cheese, however, in that the curds are not allowed to solidify, giving it a texture similar to yogurt. It is also known as fromage frais.

Ganache: A rich chocolate filling or coating made with chocolate, vegetable shortening, and possibly heavy cream. It can coat cakes or cookies, and be used as a filling for truffles.

Glaze: A liquid that gives an item a shiny surface. Examples are fruit jams that have been heated or chocolate thinned with melted vegetable shortening. Also, to cover a food with such a liquid.

Gratin: To bind together or combine food with a liquid such as cream, milk, béchamel sauce, or tomato sauce in a shallow dish. The mixture is then baked until cooked and set.

Hard-Ball Stage: In candy making, the point at which syrup has cooked long enough to form a solid ball in cold water.

Hull (also husk): To remove the leafy parts of soft fruits, such as strawberries or blackberries.

Infusion: To extract flavors by soaking them in liquid heated in a covered pan. The term also refers to the liquid resulting from this process.

Julienne: To cut into long, thin strips.

Jus: The natural juices released by roasting meats.

Larding: To inset strips of fat into pieces of meat, so that the braised meat stays moist and juicy.

Marble: To gently swirl one food into another.

Marinate: To combine food with aromatic ingredients to add flavor.

Meringue: Egg whites beaten until they are stiff, then sweetened. It can be used as the topping for pies or baked as cookies.

Muddle: To mash or crush ingredients with a spoon or a muddler (a rod with a flattened end). Usually identified with the preparation of mixed drinks.

Mull: To slowly heat cider with spices and sugar.

Parboil: To partly cook in a boiling liquid.

Peaks: The mounds made in a mixture. For example, egg white that has been whipped to stiffness. Peaks are "stiff" if they stay upright or "soft" if they curl over.

Pesto: A sauce usually made of fresh basil, garlic, olive oil, pine nuts, and cheese. The ingredients are finely chopped and then mixed, uncooked, with pasta. Generally, the term refers to any uncooked sauce made of finely chopped herbs and nuts.

Pipe: To force a semisoft food through a bag (either a pastry bag or a plastic bag with one corner cut off) to decorate food.

Pressure Cooking: To cook using steam trapped under a locked lid to produce high temperatures and achieve fast cooking time.

Purée: To mash or sieve food into a thick liquid.

Ramekin: A small baking dish used for individual servings of sweet and savory dishes.

Reduce: To cook liquids down so that some of the water evaporates.

Refresh: To pour cold water over freshly cooked vegetables to prevent further cooking and to retain color.

Rolling Boil: A boil that does not stop bubbling when stirred.

Roux: A cooked paste usually made from flour and butter, used to thicken sauces.

Satay: A dish consisting of chunks or slices of meat on bamboo skewers, which are grilled over a wood or charcoal fire, then served with spicy seasoning.

Sauté: To cook foods quickly in a small amount of oil in a skillet or sauté pan over direct heat.

Scald: To heat a liquid, usually a dairy product, until it almost boils.

Sear: To seal in a meat's juices by cooking it quickly using very high heat.

Sift: To remove large lumps from a dry ingredient such as flour or confectioners' sugar by passing it through a fine mesh. This process also incorporates air into the ingredients, making them lighter.

Simmer: To cook food in a liquid at a low enough temperature that small bubbles begin to break the surface.

Steam: To cook over boiling water in a covered pan, this method keeps foods' shape, texture, and nutritional value intact better than methods such as boiling.

Steep: To soak dry ingredients (tea leaves, ground coffee, herbs, spices, etc.) in liquid until the flavor is infused into the liquid.

Stewing: To brown small pieces of meat, poultry, or fish, then simmer them with vegetables or other ingredients in enough liquid to cover them, usually in a closed pot on the stove, in the oven, or with a slow cooker.

Thin: To reduce a mixture's thickness with the addition of more liquid.

Timbale: A large thimble or cone-shaped mold used for various sorts of food.

Truss: To use string, skewers, or pins to hold together a food to maintain its shape while it cooks (usually applied to meat or poultry).

Unleavened: Baked goods that contain no agents to give them volume, such as baking powder, baking soda, or yeast.

Vinaigrette: A general term referring to any sauce made with vinegar, oil, and seasonings.

Zest: The thin, brightly colored outer part of the rind of citrus fruits. It contains volatile oils, used as a flavoring.

Recipe Index

Reader Feedback Form

Dear Reader,

We are very interested in what our readers think. Please fill in the form below and return it to:

Whispering Pine Press International, Inc.
c/o Blueberry Delights Cookbook
P.O. Box 214, Spokane Valley, WA 99037-0214 USA
Phone: (509) 928-8700 | Fax: (509) 922-9949
Email: sales@WhisperingPinePress.com
Publisher Website: www.WhisperingPinePress.com
Book Website: www.BlueberryDelightsCookbook.com

Name: _____

Address: _____

City, St., Zip: _____

Phone/Fax: (____) _____ / (____) _____

Email: _____

Comments/Suggestions: _____

_____

_____

_____

_____

A great deal of care and attention has been exercised in the creation of this book. Designing a great cookbook that is original, fun, and easy to use has been a job that required many hours of diligence, creativity, and research. Although we strive to make this book completely error free, errors and discrepancies may not be completely excluded. If you come across any errors or discrepancies, please make a note of them and send them to our publishing office. We are constantly updating our manuscripts, eliminating errors, and improving quality.

Please contact us at the address above.

About the Cookbook Delights Series

The *Cookbook Delights Series* includes many different topics and themes. If you have a passion for food and wish to know more information about different foods, then this series of cookbooks will be beneficial to you. Each book features a different type of food, such as avocados, strawberries, huckleberries, salmon, vegetarian, lentils, almonds, cherries, coconuts, lemons, and many, many more.

The *Cookbook Delights Series* not only includes cookbooks about individual foods but also includes several holiday-themed cookbooks. Whatever your favorite holiday may be, chances are we have a cookbook with recipes designed with that holiday in mind. Some examples include *Halloween Delights, Thanksgiving Delights, Christmas Delights, Valentine Delights, Mother's Day Delights, St. Patrick's Day Delights,* and *Easter Delights.*

Each cookbook is designed for easy use and is organized into alphabetical sections. Over 250 recipes are included along with other interesting facts, folklore, and history of the featured food or theme. Each book comes with a beautiful full-color cover, ordering information, and a list of other upcoming books in the series.

Note cards, bookmarks, and a daily journal have been printed and are available to go along with each cookbook. You may view the entire line of cookbooks, journals, cards, posters, puzzles, and bookmarks by visiting our websites at www.CookBookDelights.net and www.BlueberryDelights.com, or you can email us with your questions and your comments to: Sales@WhisperingPinePress.com.

Please ask your local bookstore to carry these sets of books. To order, please contact:

Whispering Pine Press International, Inc.
c/o Blueberry Delights Cookbook
P.O. Box 214, Spokane Valley, WA 99037-0214 USA
Phone: (509) 9928-8700| Fax: (509) 922-9949
Email: sales@WhisperingPinePress.com
Publisher Website: www.WhisperingPinePress.com
Book Website: www.BlueberryDelightsCookbook.com
SAN 253-200X

We Invite You to Join the Whispering Pine Press International, Inc., Book Club!

Whispering Pine Press International, Inc.
c/o Blueberry Delights Cookbook
P.O. Box 214, Spokane Valley, WA 99037-0214 USA
Phone: (509) 928-8700l Fax: (509) 922-9949
Email: sales@WhisperingPinePress.com
Publisher Website: www.WhisperingPinePress.com
Book Website: www.BlueberryDelightsCookbook.com

Buy 11 books and get the next one free, based on the average price of the first eleven purchased.

How the club works:

Simply use the order form below and order books from our catalog. You can buy just one at a time or all eleven at once. After the first eleven books are purchased, the next one is free. Please add shipping and handling as listed on this form. There are no purchase requirements at any time during your membership. Free book credit is based on the average price of the first eleven books purchased.

Join today! Pick your books and mail in the form today!

Yes! I want to join the Whispering Pine Press International, Inc., Book Club! Enroll me and send the books indicated below.

Title   Price

1. _____
2. _____
3. _____
4. _____
5. _____
6. _____
7. _____
8. _____
9. _____
10. _____
11. _____

Free Book Title: _____
Free Book Price: _____ Avg. Price: _____ Total Price: _____
Credit for the free book is based on the average price of the first 11 books purchased.
(Circle one) Check | Visa | MasterCard | Discover | American Express
Credit Card #: _____ Expiration Date: _____
Name: _____
Address: _____
City: _____State: _____Country: _____
Zip/Postal: _____Phone: (_____) _____
Email: _____

Signature_____

Whispering Pine Press International, Inc.
Fundraising Opportunities

Fundraising cookbooks are proven moneymakers and great keepsake providers for your group. Whispering Pine Press International, Inc., offers a very special personalized cookbook fundraising program that encourages success to organizations all across the USA.

Our prices are competitive and fair. Currently, we offer a special of 100 books with many free features and excellent customer service. Any purchase you make is guaranteed first-rate.

Flexibility is not a problem. If you have special needs, we guarantee our cooperation in meeting each of them. Our goal is to create a cookbook that goes beyond your expectations. We have the confidence and a record that promises continual success.

Another great fundraising program is the *Cookbook Delights Series* Program. With cookbook orders of 50 copies or more, your organization receives a huge discount, making for a prompt and lucrative solution.

We also specialize in assisting group fundraising – Christian, community, nonprofit, and academic among them. If you are struggling for a new idea, something that will enhance your success and broaden your appeal, Whispering Pine Press International, Inc., can help.

For more information, write, phone, or fax to:

Whispering Pine Press International, Inc.
P.O. Box 214, Spokane Valley, WA 99037-0214 USA
Phone: (509) 928-8700 | Fax: (509) 922-9949
Email: sales@WhisperingPinePress.com
Publisher Website: www.WhisperingPinePress.com
Book Website: www.BlueberryDelightsCookbook.com
SAN 253-200X

Personalized and/or Translated Order Form
for Any Book by
Whispering Pine Press International, Inc.

Dear Readers:

If you or your organization wishes to have this book or any other of our books personalized, we will gladly accommodate your needs. For instance, if you would like to change the names of the characters in a book to the names of the children in your family or Sunday school class, we would be happy to work with you on such a project. We can add more information of your choosing and customize this book especially for your family, group, or organization.

We are also offering an option of translating your book into another language. Please fill out the form below telling us exactly how you would like us to personalize your book.

Please send your request to:
Whispering Pine Press International, Inc.
P.O. Box 214, Spokane Valley, WA 99037-0214 USA
Phone: (509) 928-8700 | Fax: (509) 922-9949
Email: sales@WhisperingPinePress.com
Publisher Website: www.WhisperingPinePress.com
Book Website: www.BlueberryDelightsCookbook.com

Person/Organization placing request: _____

Date_____ Phone: (____) _____

Address_____ Fax: (____) _____

City_____ State_____ Zip: _____

Language of the book: _____

Please explain your request in detail: _____

_____

_____

_____

_____

_____

Blueberry Delights Cookbook

A Collection of Blueberry Recipes

How to Order

Get your additional copies of this book by returning an order form and your check, money order, or credit card information to:

Whispering Pine Press International, Inc.
P.O. Box 214, Spokane Valley, WA 99037-0214 USA
Phone: (509) 928-8700 | Fax: (509) 922-9949
Email: sales@WhisperingPinePress.com
Publisher Website: www.WhisperingPinePress.com
Book Website: www.BlueberryDelightsCookbook.com

Customer Name: _____

Address: _____

City, St., Zip: _____

Phone/Fax: _____

Email: _____

- -

Please send me_____ copies of_____

_____ at $_____

per copy and $4.95 for shipping and handling per book, plus $2.95 each for additional books. Enclosed is my check, money order, or charge my account for $_____.

☐ Check   ☐ Money Order   ☐ Credit Card

(*Circle One*) MasterCard | Discover | Visa | American Express

☐ ☐ ☐ ☐   ☐ ☐ ☐ ☐   ☐ ☐ ☐ ☐   ☐ ☐ ☐ ☐

Expiration Date: _____

_____
Signature

_____
Print Name

Whispering Pine Press International, Inc. Order Form

Gift-wrapping, Autographing, and Inscription

We are proud to offer personal autographing by the author. For a limited time this service is absolutely free!
Gift-wrapping is also available for $4.95 per item.

1. Sold To

Name: _____
Street/Route: _____
_____
City: _____
State: _____ Zip: _____
Country: _____
Gift message: _____
_____
Email address: _____
Daytime Phone: (_ _) _ _ _-_ _ _ _
*Necessary for verifying orders
Home Phone: (_ _) _ _ _-_ _ _ _
Fax: (_ _) _ _ _-_ _ _ _

2. Ship To

☐ Is this a new or corrected address?

☐ Alternative Shipping Address

☐ Mailing Address

Name: _____
Address: _____
_____
City: _____
State: _____ Zip: _____
Country: _____
Email address: _____

3. Items Ordered

ISBN # /Item #	Size	Color	Qty.	Title or Description	Price	Total

4. Method Of Payment

International, Inc. (No Cash or COD's)

☐ Visa ☐ MasterCard ☐ Discover ☐ American Express ☐ Check/Money Order

Please make it payable to Whispering Pine Press International, Inc. (No Cash or COD's)

Account Number   Expiration Date
_____ / _____
Month Year

☐☐☐☐ ☐☐☐☐ ☐☐☐☐ ☐☐☐☐

Signature_____
Cardholder's signature

Printed Name_____
Please print name of cardholder

Address of Cardholder_____

Subtotal	
Gift wrap $4.95 Each	
For delivery in WA add 8.7% sales tax.	
Shipping See chart at left	
6. Total	

5. Shipping & Handling

Continental US

US Postal Ground: For books please add $4.95 for the first book and $2.95 each for additional books.
All non-book items, add 15% of the Subtotal.
Please allow 1-4 weeks for delivery.
US Postal Air: Please add $15.00 shipping and handling.
Please allow 1-3 days for delivery.
Alaska, Hawaii, and the US Territories By Ship:
Please add 10% shipping and handling
(minimum charge $15.00).

Please
By Air: Please add 12% shipping and handling (minimum charge $15.00).
Please allow 2 –6 weeks for delivery.
International By Ship: Please add 10% shipping and handling (minimum charge $15.00).
Please allow 6-12 weeks for delivery.
By Air: Please add 12% shipping and handling (minimum charge $15.00).
Please allow 2-6 weeks for delivery.
FedEx Shipments: Add $5.00 to the above airmail charges for overnight delivery.

Shop Online:
www.whisperingpinepress.com
Fax orders to: (509) 922-9949

Whispering Pine Press International, Inc.
P.O. Box 214
Spokane Valley, WA 99037-0214 USA
Phone: (509) 928-8700 • Fax: (509) 922-9949
Email: sales@whisperingpinepress.com
Website: www.whisperingpinepress.com

About the Author and Cook

Karen Jean Matsko Hood has always enjoyed cooking, baking, and experimenting with recipes. At this time Hood is working to complete a series of cookbooks that blends her skills and experience in cooking and entertaining. Hood entertains large groups of people and especially enjoys designing creative menus with holiday, international, ethnic, and regional themes.

Hood is publishing a cookbook series entitled the *Cookbook Delights Series*, in which each cookbook emphasizes a different food ingredient or theme. The first cookbook in the series is *Apple Delights Cookbook*. Hood is working to complete another series of cookbooks titled *Hood and Matsko Family Cookbooks*, which includes many recipes handed down from her family heritage and others that have emerged from more current family traditions. She has been invited to speak on talk radio shows on various topics, and favorite recipes from her cookbooks have been prepared on local television programs.

Hood was born and raised in Great Falls, Montana. As an undergraduate, she attended the College of St. Benedict in St. Joseph, Minnesota, and St. John's University in Collegeville, Minnesota. She attended the University of Great Falls in Great Falls, Montana. Hood received a B.S. Degree in Natural Science from the College of St. Benedict and minored in both Psychology and Secondary Education. Upon her graduation, Hood and her husband taught science and math on the island of St. Croix in the U.S. Virgin Islands. Hood has completed postgraduate classes at the University of Iowa in Iowa City, Iowa. In May 2001, she completed her Master's Degree in Pastoral Ministry at Gonzaga University in Spokane, Washington. She has taken postgraduate classes at Lewis and Clark College on the North Idaho college campus in Coeur d'Alene, Idaho, Taylor University in Fort Wayne, Indiana, Spokane Falls Community College, Spokane Community College, Washington State University, University of Washington, and Eastern Washington University. Hood is working on research projects to complete her Ph.D. in Leadership Studies at Gonzaga University in Spokane, Washington.

Hood resides in Greenacres, Washington, along with her husband, many of her sixteen children, and foster children. Her interests include writing, research, and teaching. She previously has volunteered as a court advocate in the Spokane juvenile court system for abused and neglected children. Hood is a literary advocate for youth and adults. Her hobbies include cooking, baking, collecting, photography, indoor and outdoor gardening, farming, and the cultivation of unusual flowering plants and orchids. She enjoys raising several specialty breeds of animals including Babydoll Southdown, Friesen, and Icelandic sheep, Icelandic horses, bichons frisés, cockapoos, Icelandic sheepdogs, a Newfoundland, a Rottweiler, a variety of Nubian and fainting goats, and a few rescue cats. Hood also enjoys bird-watching and finds all aspects of nature precious.

She demonstrates a passionate appreciation of the environment and a respect for all life. She also invites you to visit her websites:

www.KarenJeanMatskoHood.com
www.KarenJeanMatskoHoodBookstore.com
www.KarenJeanMatskoHoodBlog.com
www.KarensKidsBooks.com
www.KarensTeenBooks.com

www.HoodFamilyBlog.com
www.HoodFamily.com

Author's Social Media
Please Follow the Author on **Twitter**: @KarenJeanHood
Friend her on **Facebook**: Karen Jean Matsko Hood Author Fan Page
Google Plus Profile: Karen Jean Matsko Hood
Pinterest.com/KarenJMHood

www.ingramcontent.com/pod-product-compliance
Lightning Source LLC
Chambersburg PA
CBHW031235090426
42742CB00007B/205